It All Started in Kindergarten

Unforgettable Stories for Listening and Conversation

Gail Feinstein Forman
San Diego Community College District

Based on Robert Fulghum's books
All I Need to Know I Learned in Kindergarten
and It Was on Fire When I Lay Down on It

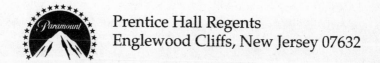
Prentice Hall Regents
Englewood Cliffs, New Jersey 07632

Library of Congress Cataloging-in-Publication Data

Forman, Gail Feinstein.
    It all started in kindergarten : unforgettable stories for
listening and conversation / Gail Feinstein Forman.
        p.   cm.
    "Based on Robert Fulghum's books, All I need to know I learned in
kindergarten and It was on fire when I lay down on it."
    ISBN 0-13-630971-2
    1. English language—Textbooks for foreign speakers.   2. Readers.
I. Fulghum, Robert.   All I need to know I learned in Kindergarten.
II. Fulghum, Robert.   It was on fire when I lay down on it.
III. Title.
PE1128.F584   1994
428.6`4—dc20   94-5470
                                                                   CIP

Acquistions Editor: Nancy Leonhardt
Production Editor: Janet Johnston
Desk-top Composition and Page Make-up: Jan Sivertsen
Director of Production and Manufacturing: David Riccardi
Editorial Production/Design Manager: Dominick Mosco
Production Coordinator: Ray Keating
Illustrator: Maxine Ann Sorokin
Cover Coordinator: Merle Krumper
Cover Designer: Rosemarie Paccione

Permission to reproduce audio excerpts from *All I Need to Know I Learned in Kindergarten* and *It Was On Fire When I Lay Down On It* granted by Random House Audio Publishing Inc.

Permission to reproduce printed excerpts from *All I Need to Know I Learned in Kindergarten* and *It Was On Fire When I Lay Down On It* granted by Villard Books, a division of Random House Audio Publishing, Inc.

© 1994 by PRENTICE HALL REGENTS
Prentice-Hall, Inc.
A Paramount Communications Company
Englewood Cliffs, New Jersey 07632

Printed in the United States of America

10   9   8   7   6   5   4   3   2   1

ISBN 0-13-630971-2

Prentice-Hall International (UK) Limited, *London*
Prentice-Hall of Australia Pty. Limited, *Sydney*
Prentice-Hall Canada Inc., *Toronto*
Prentice-Hall Hispanoamericana, S.A., *Mexico*
Prentice-Hall of India Private Limited, *New Delhi*
Prentice-Hall of Japan, Inc., *Tokyo*
Simon & Schuster Asia Pte. Ltd., *Singapore*
Editora Prentice-Hall do Brasil, Ltda., *Rio de Janeiro*

Printed on Recycled Paper

Dedication

To Yaakov—for all we've shared

CONTENTS

FOREWORD
From the author of the essays to the reader

When I was a child in school I was always happy when my class went on an adventure away from the school to learn something about the world. This is called "going on a field trip." At those times we visited a fire station, a bakery, the mayor's office, and a dairy. When we returned to school we would draw pictures and write stories about our experiences.

Even though I am now an adult, I realize that I am still doing what I did in school. First, I go out in the world to listen and look. I take careful notes. When I come home I turn these experiences into stories that are collected in books. My books have now been translated into twenty-four languages and are sold in 94 countries.

When I have wandered outside my own country in search of stories, I have found it difficult sometimes to understand what was going on because I did not speak the language. How I regret that! I understand how important it is to speak more than one language. I know how hard it is to learn even a little bit of another language, for I have often tried.

That is why I am glad my stories are being used to help you learn English. If we can speak to one another in a common language, we can understand one another. If we understand one another, the world will become a better place in which to live. I hope you understand my stories. I wish I could hear and understand yours. I wish you good luck and send my best regards.

Robert Fulghum
Seattle, Washington
January 1993

PREFACE

Mai, a very bright but reticent Chinese student, came up to talk to me after our English class had finished.

Mai:	"Teacher, can I ask you a question?"
Teacher:	"Sure. What is it?"
Mai:	"Well, I want to ask you if the idiom we studied today, 'going from the frying pan into the fire,' has a meaning similar to 'It was on fire when I lay down on it.'"

At first, I was taken aback by her astute observation. I was also surprised at her unusually bold behavior of approaching me face-to-face. She had sat in my class an entire semester, and this was the first time she had ever asked me any questions!

Teacher:	"I'm surprised you remember the idiom about the burning bed! We studied it five months ago."
Mai:	"Oh yes, teacher. I loved the story. It was real life."

A few weeks before that, a similarly quiet, elderly Vietnamese student, who had arrived in class early, was feverishly writing, then checking another paper, then writing again.

Teacher:	"Hanh, it looks like you're working on a big project."
Hanh:	"Yes, teacher. I've almost finished. Almost."

Respecting my student's privacy, I decided not to ask any more about this "project". Instead, I surreptiously looked at the paper she was checking and saw that it was Fulghum's title essay from his *All I Really Need To Know I Learned In Kindergarten*, which I had used in class two months before. She was translating it from English to Vietnamese!

And so it went. Every once in a while, a student would make reference to a word or idea contained in the Fulghum essays that I had used in class the previous semester. After teaching ESL for ten years, I seemed to have finally hit upon some study material with magical universal appeal; students from many cultures in my class not only related to the essays but remembered their contents and learned from them. I wanted to make Fulghum's essays available and accessible to an even larger audience of English language students. I promised myself that I'd get back to this "someday" and develop the material further. This book is the result of that promise.

This promise could never have been fulfilled without the help and support of many giving people. First and foremost, I must offer giant-size balloons of gratitude to Robert Fulghum, who sustained my belief in miracles through our telephone conversations and through his successful efforts at Divine intervention. To borrow a phrase from the Chinese, "Ten thousand thank you's!!"

For professional encouragement, I must thank Leann Howard for scribbling "Go for it" on all my teaching and program proposals. Thank you's also go to Gretchen Bitterlin for always taking the time to advise on class and program activities, and to

Roberta Alexander for offering me the most recent floor for teaching exploration. An additional note of thanks to Robert Walsh for starting and encouraging me "on the road" to ESL. Also, I must include a thank you to Linda Sheldon at Random House for finding a way to make this book happen. For the actual production of this book, I must thank many at Prentice Hall—Nancy Leonhardt and Terry TenBarge for patience and advice throughout this circuitous process, Janet Johnston for belief in this project and excellent editorial advice. Also, thanks to Ken Clinton and Tom Dare for patiently and consistently following through on their marketing suggestions, and Jan Sivertsen for great creativity and resilience in the design and page layout of this book.

Friendship of a special few has helped guide this particular being along myriad paths. Margo N. Tighe, tea-drinker extraordinaire, shared her thousand-cup teapot at every step along the continuum and picked me up from her floor when the occasion arose. A "Toda Raba" to Annette Segal, the quintessential model and shaper of the phrase "Do It!," who shared with me the joys and discovery of the limitless possibilities within us and led me into the twentieth century with the Mac and a telephone-answering machine. Thanks to Maxine Sorokin, the book's illustrator and my good friend, whose conversations and pictures inspired me. Also, in the friendship category, special note to Dr. Sheldon Hendler for his perception and direction to break through circles. To Dr. Matt Van Ben Schoten, whose work has expanded my realm of the possible. And to Burt, Ellen, and Jeanne Bialik for years of valued friendship and for presenting us with our first copy of *It Was on Fire When I Lay Down On It*. And to former student and friend, Phu Luong, for providing me with a continous example of insight and courage and for generously teaching and sharing the ways of T'ai Chi.

My family played a great role in getting me to this place in life. Special thanks to my mother and father who I think knew this book might come about one day. To my grandfather "Pop," who left us the legacy of how to "make the best." To my cousin Judi Cooper, for cartwheels and support over many, many moons! To all my aunts and uncles, especially to Bill and Kay Boyd, for their encouragement and assistance in both our California and New Jersey life. To my brother Mark and his wife, Jo Anne, for helping us make a permanent home in California. A special mention must go to Yetta and Morris Gelber for becoming an important part of our family.

And to my husband, Jack, who equally shared in the birth of this book, for his flexibility, humor and understanding over our twenty-two years together.

Anna, in the *The King and I,* aptly states that "when you become a teacher, by your students you'll be taught". To every student who walked through the doors of my classroom, for sharing your stories and yourself, **Thank you**.

TO THE TEACHER: SUGGESTIONS FOR USING THE TEXT

What Is *It All Started In Kindergarten*?

It All Started in Kindergarten is a unique ESL audio tape–text program. It is the first book in a two-book ESL series based on best-selling author Robert Fulghum's books *All I Need to Know I Learned in Kindergarten* and *It Was on Fire When I Lay Down on It*. It is designed for high beginning–intermediate students seeking engaging and challenging materials to strengthen communicative English language skills, particularly listening and conversation. The program is appropriate for both ESL and bilingual interactive skill courses in high school, college, and adult education.

The book consists of ten chapters, each centered around a universal theme contained in one Fulghum essay. A variety of communicative exercises are provided for students on each essay's topics that are relevant to their own experiences. Great emphasis is placed on cross-cultural issues, which are examined in several sections throughout each chapter. In addition, students will be introduced to and will be asked to practice language techniques in the major academic skill areas of taking notes, reporting information, and drawing conclusions.

Why an ESL Text with a Listening Focus?

Research into the methods of second language acquisition demonstrates that although listening is the most frequently used language skill, it is often given much too little emphasis in many ESL classrooms. Listening skills need to be seen as an active, not passive, skill area and should be part of the curriculum in order to improve comprehensive language understanding inside and outside the classroom.

This text and tape program was designed to develop ESL students' listening comprehension skills by using the basic principles of "focused listening." In "focused listening" exercises, students are asked to determine what the main ideas of the listening passage are or to find specific information about something contained in the passage. Students demonstrate their comprehension by answering a series of questions about that passage. They practice listening for a specific purpose by training themselves to focus only on the content necessary to meet that goal.

Chapters are self-contained and therefore can be taught in any order. It is recommended, however, that the first and second chapters be taught first because each contains detailed instructions for using each chapter section. These chapters contain the introductory sections on note-taking, reporting information and drawing conclusions. Teaching these chapters first will also help familiarize both the students and the instructor with the format and goals of succeeding chapters.

Each chapter consists of five sections, each of which contains separate teaching instructions for that segment. Additional suggestions for methodology are provided in the following outline of chapter divisions.

1. Chapter Preview

Each chapter opens with an illustration page and a quotation related to the chapter theme. The illustrations are designed to be fairly open-ended and sometimes have more than one possible interpretation; this open-endedness is intended to challenge students' imaginations and stimulate class discussion. The page following the illustration offers a brief text further developing the chapter theme.

Partner interviews follow with oral and written cooperative group exercises reinforcing the language of the student responses. Teachers are requested to collect these group writings. They can then be shared with the class in many ways - put on the board, read by other students, etc. They can be graded or ungraded.

Teachers are encouraged to use these preview exerecises as warm-ups for the essay and exercises that follow. In addition, they can be used to reinforce sentence structures being practiced in class.

2. Vocabulary Preview and Quick-Check Section

This section consists of exercises to introduce and practice key vocabulary words and phrases that students will hear on the tape. **Vocabulary definitions are given according to their usage in each specific story.** With the definitions are sample sentences that are usually taken directly from the essay itself and that reflect how the vocabulary is used in the essay. The Vocabulary Quick-Check Review consists of a matching exercise to test the comprehension of the new vocabulary.

3. Essay Preview

This section contains a brief introduction to the essay contents. It can be used as an additional warm-up and refocusing exercise for the essay.

4. Focused Listening

Students are provided many opportunities to be actively engaged in listening comprehension activities. Focused Listening exercises include:

a. <u>What's This Story About?</u>—Students focus on the content and details by answering multiple choice questions about the essay.

b. <u>Listen Again</u>—Students listen to the complete essay again with no stops or interruptions. They are then asked to change incorrect statements about the essay to correct ones.

Note: The complete text of each essay appears in the back of this book, and it can be valuable for content or vocabulary review. It is advised, however, that students refer to the written text only after the listening exercises have been completed.

5. Class Activities

In these interactive skill exercises, students can work individually, in pairs, or in groups. Exercises in this section can lay the foundation for more in-depth discussion of issues raised throughout the essay, and they encourage use of additional materials related to these issues. There are many opportunities here for sharing stories, as well as for oral presentations or writing exercises about particular stories the students like.

The Class Activity sections are divided into four parts:

1. <u>What Do You Think?</u> Students answer questions about the essay orally or on paper. These questions are formulated to develop cross-cultural connections with the main ideas of the essay theme.

2. <u>Reflections</u> This section provides students with readings and ideas for additional cross-cultural comparisons on theme-related issues.

3. <u>Dictation</u> Students listen to a segment of the tape for dictation practice and fill in the missing words.

4. <u>Speaking of Culture</u> This section permits students to eavesdrop on conversations that demonstrate U.S. attitudes on the chapter theme compared with or contrasted to the attitudes of other societies on similar issues. Questions for discussion follow.

Why Use Robert Fulghum's Material in ESL Classrooms?

The books of Robert Fulghum—minister, teacher, fiddler, and artist—have reached an extraordinarily large and diverse national and international audience. His books have topped best-seller lists for three years in a row and have been translated into more than twenty languages.

The main reasons Fulghum's essays are ideal source materials for ESL programs are the same reasons these books have achieved international recognition.

First, Fulghum's themes are truly universal. The "everyman" tales of his successes and failures cut across all cultural boundaries and can be understood by everyone. These short "slices of life" reflect the author's obsession with what he calls "exploring the meaning <u>in</u> life rather than <u>of</u> life." The stories are related with a unique blend of humor, honesty, and pathos; it is not surprising that so many people are so easily drawn to his writings. The universality of the themes—such as love, friendship, and personal dreams—will keep these stories fresh for many years to come, and this universality will expose ESL students to the ideas and expressive writing style of one of America's most popular writers.

Another reason the essays are so well suited for ESL materials is that they are told in colorful, everyday language easily understood by non-native speakers. In addition, Fulghum's personal reading style on the audio tapes is unusually clear and engaging. He creates an instant bond with his audience. Listeners feel as if he were talking directly to each of them. They are pulled into his narratives immediately, often feeling they too have shared the experience. The stories become immediate "hooks," motivating students to concentrate on content, not only on form —an essential skill for the development of listening comprehension.

Finally, Fulghum's short essays are almost certain to have a personal impact on ESL students. The essays selected for this book are about remarkable, inspiring people and events. No matter what difficulties Fulghum's characters face, there is always hope and optimism—or a life lesson to take home with you.

I have tried to provide class activities that stimulate the creative juices of both the students and the teacher. Feel free to adapt any of the suggested ideas to your own style—or create your own ideas. Based on my personal and classroom experience with Fulghum's essays, I feel confident that they will have a lasting impression both on your class and on yourself.

Have fun!

The time has come,

The walrus said,

To talk of many things

Of shoes and ships and sealing wax

And whether pigs have wings.

—Lewis J. Carroll
The Walrus and the Carpenter

Chapter 1

IT ALL STARTED IN KINDERGARTEN

*Remember the little seed in the plastic cup:
the roots go down and the plant goes up
and nobody knows how or why, but we
are all like that.*

—Robert Fulghum,
<u>All I Need to Know I
Learned in Kindergarten</u>

*L*ook at the chapter, the picture, the title, and the quotation above the picture. What do you think this chapter is about? What does the picture tell you about the subject?

*C*hapter Preview

About Early Life Lessons

It's fun to share memories about your childhood and early school years. Since many of your classmates have very different cultural and educational backgrounds from yours, the English class provides a great opportunity for you to share this special part of your personal life story.

In this chapter, you will interview a classmate about either his or her earliest school memories or earliest lessons that he or she learned as a child. You will ask your partner questions about his or her childhood and take notes about the answers. Throughout the chapters in this book, you will be asked to take notes and report your information to the class. Before you get ready to interview your partner, let's take a look at the ideas and skills of taking notes.

What Is "Taking Notes"?

When you take notes, you write down only a few words or ideas about the main idea of a conversation, speech, or article. You do not write every word that is spoken or read. It is very helpful to develop this skill. It saves time when you are reading a lot of information at one time or listening to someone else telling this information to you. It also trains you to focus on only the main ideas of what someone says, so you will not feel confused if you don't understand every word in the conversation.

In addition, there are other benefits for both you and your partner. Your partner will be able to speak freely and naturally, and he or she won't have to stop and wait for you to write down every word that is said. Also, you will be practicing your listening skills at the same time as thinking and writing quickly in English.

What situations can you think of in which the skill of taking notes would be very helpful? Have you had any experience of taking notes in English? Have you had any experience of taking notes in your language? Tell your class about these experiences.

How to Take Notes

The first important thing to learn about taking notes is that there is **more than one way** to take notes. In time, you will develop your own style although the basic form is similar for everyone. Keep these ideas in your mind when you take notes:

1. Be a good listener. Be open to your partner's ideas and enjoy learning about each other.

2. Ask questions if you don't understand something you heard.

3. Learn to listen for the main idea of what someone is saying.

4. Write down only information about the main ideas of the speaker.

5. Don't worry about writing complete sentences. A few words that will remind you of the information is all you really need.

6. Don't be concerned about grammar, spelling, or punctuation in your notes. If you give an oral or written report later about the interview, you will have a lot of time to change your work then.

7. Remember that learning a new skill takes time and that practicing improves your skills.

EXAMPLES OF TAKING NOTES

Kwang and Ari are students in the same ESL class. The teacher has asked Kwang and Ari to be partners and to interview each other and practice taking notes. First, Kwang will interview Ari and take notes on what Ari says:

Kwang: Ari, what was your favorite activity in elementary school?

Ari: Well, let me see. I think my favorite activity was playing soccer on the school playground.

(Kwang takes notes and writes: **Favorite activity—soccer**)

Kwang: Ari, what do you remember about your first day of school?

Ari: Right now I can't think of anything!

Kwang: That's OK. How about a memory about a favorite holiday celebration instead?

Ari: That's easy to remember. New Year's Day was always my favorite day of the year. All the relatives got together and ate, sang, danced, and played games until midnight. These are memories I will always keep close to my heart.

(Kwang writes: **Best holiday memories—New Years Day—family fun —stay up late—eat and dance.**)

How would **you** take notes about Ari's conversation with Kwang? Write your notes here:

1. _____

2. _____

Compare your answers with your classmates' answers.

Interviewing Your Partner

Now it's your turn.

Sit in groups of four students. Name each member of the group in the following way: Student A, Student B, Student C, and Student D. Students A and B should interview each other. Students C and D should interview each other.

Ask your partner the following interview questions and take notes on the answers.

1. What were your favorite activities in elementary school or when you were a child?

   _____

   _____

2. What do you remember about your first day of school or a special holiday celebration at home?

   _____

   _____

3. Can you remember the name of your first teacher? If yes, what was her or his name? If not, what was the name of your closest childhood friend?

_____

_____

4. What things do you remember learning in your first teacher's class?

_____

_____

5. When you were a child, was there another person who taught you special lessons that you have always remembered? If yes, who was this person? What lessons did he or she teach you?

_____

_____

Reporting Your Information to the Group

Read over the notes you took about your partner's early life. Then tell the group all about your partner's early life.

Examples:

a. (Ben reports about Sonia) "Sonia's favorite activity in elementary school was lunch time. She remembers she was very afraid the first day of school."

b. (Maria reports about Nate) "Nate doesn't remember the name of his first teacher, but he remembers she had red hair. He said he remembers this teacher because she taught him to love to read."

Writing the Group Report

Now that you have heard some information about each group member, your group will work together on a short writing project. This is a group project: each member will have a specific job to do, and there will be a specific time in which to complete the project.

The group project is to write two sentences about each student in the group. These sentences will describe something you learned about each person from the interview reports. You will have 25 minutes to complete the project. Each group member will share his or her ideas about what to write, and then each group will choose a group reporter.

Here are the jobs for each group member.

Student A (<u>Recorder</u>): Writes down the sentences the group decides to write on just one piece of paper.

Student B (<u>Conversation Leader</u>): Makes sure every student in the group speaks up about his or her ideas. Student B asks each student to give his or her opinion about what to write.

Student C (<u>Timekeeper</u>): Watches the time and makes sure the conversation keeps moving forward. Student C reminds the other students about the time they have left to complete the project. If Student C sees that the group needs more time, he or she will ask the teacher for extra time.

Student D (<u>Checker</u>): Checks the sentences for spelling and punctuation after they are all written. Student D then reads the sentences to the group. If the group is satisfied with the sentences, Student D asks each student to sign his or her name on the bottom of the paper. Student D tells the group reporter that the group in ready, and the reporter reports the results of the interviews to the whole class. After telling the report to the class, the reporter will hand in the group report paper to the instructor.

$\mathcal{V}$ocabulary Preview

Words and Phrases

Before listening to the essay, let's preview some specific vocabulary words you will hear. In this section, each new vocabulary word is listed with its definition beside it. In addition, a sample sentence containing the new word or words follows the definition. In many cases, the sample sentences are taken directly from the essay you will hear. These sentences are marked with quotation marks (" . . . ").

WORDS or PHRASES	MEANING
1. credo	a statement that describes what a person believes and thinks is true about life (Example: "Each spring, for many years, I have set myself the task of writing a personal statement of belief: a **credo**.")
2. wisdom	to be wise and have knowledge about something (Example: "**Wisdom** was not at the top of the graduate-school mountain, but there in the sandpile [a small area for children to play in the sand] in Sunday School [schools run by churches and temples to teach the custom and beliefs of its religion to children] . . .")
3. flush	to pull down the handle after using the toilet (Example: "Parents always remind their children to **flush** after using the toilet.")
4. to stick together (idiom)	to stay together with other people, usually for cooperation and support (Example: "When you go out into the world, watch out for traffic, hold hands, and **stick together**.")
5. wonder	excitement and amazement about something (Example: "Be aware of **wonder**.")

WORDS or PHRASES	MEANING
6. Styrofoam	a thick, white form of plastic, often used to make drinking cups for hot drinks
	(Example: "Remember the little seed in the **Styrofoam** cup: the roots go down and the plant goes up, and nobody really knows why or how . . . ")
7. Dick and Jane	the names of two main characters who appeared in elementary reading books for English-speaking children during the 1940s and 1950s
	(Example: "And then remember the **Dick-and-Jane** books and the first word you learned—the biggest word of all— LOOK.")
8. the Golden Rule	a proverb that advises everyone to treat other people the way you would like to have them treat you
	(Example: "Parents and teachers think **The Golden Rule** is an important rule for children to learn early in life.")
9. ecology	a science that studies the relationships of all living things with their environment
	(Example: "We must pay attention to keeping the **ecology** of the earth in balance.")
10. sane	a description of something that is practical and makes sense
	(Example: "We need **sane** policies to protect the earth.")

Vocabulary Quick-Check Review

Check your understanding of the new words and phrases introduced in this chapter by matching the words in Column A with their closest definition in Column B.

Example:

Column A		**Column B**
__b__ kindergarten	a.	area filled with sand for children to play in
__a__ sandpile	b.	first year in school

Column A		**Column B**
1. ____ wisdom	a.	amazement
2. ____ Golden Rule	b.	study of environment
3. ____ flush	c.	belief
4. ____ credo	d.	practical and sensible
5. ____ Dick and Jane	e.	stay together
6. ____ Styrofoam	f.	knowledge
7. ____ wonder	g.	treat people in a good way
8. ____ stick together	h.	boy and girl in reading book
9. ____ sane	i.	kind of plastic
10. ____ ecology	j.	pull handle on toilet

*E*ssay Preview

Would you like to hear a popular essay (a composition about one person's ideas or opinions on a subject) that has been translated into more than 24 languages? Robert Fulghum wrote this essay in 1985 when he was a minister in Seattle, Washington. He read it to people in his church, and they loved it! Many people asked Fulghum for a copy of it to send to other friends and family. The interest in this essay grew all around the world.

In this essay, Fulghum describes his philosophy of life. He believes that life is simpler than most people think. He thinks we can change and improve the world if people would just follow the basic life lessons we learned in kindergarten. Thousands of people enjoyed Fulghum's message and found some truth in his words. Let's see what you think.

$\mathcal{F}$ocused Listening

Look over the following questions before you listen to the tape. This will give you an idea of what information to focus on while listening to the essay the first time. The title and the section of each part you will listen to will be announced on the tape. Listen carefully to each listening section, and then circle the correct answer for each question in that section.

Example: The name of this chapter is:
  a. It All Started In Kindergarten
  b. My First Teacher

Which one did you circle, *a* or *b*? Check with your classmates. That's right. The correct answer is *a*.

Now you try. Circle the correct answer.

What's This Story About?

SECTION A

1. Where did Fulghum say he learned all about life?
    a. In his backyard.
    b. In kindergarten.

2. Which two rules did Fulghum learn while in kindergarten?
    a. Don't take things that aren't yours, and say you're sorry if you hurt someone.
    b. Take showers, and remember to take things that don't belong to you.

3. Fulghum says that to live a balanced life you should
    a. learn how to lift weights.
    b. draw, sing, and dance every day.

4. Fulghum advises us to
    a. swim every afternoon.
    b. take a nap every afternoon.

SECTION B

5. When you go out into the world, it's best
    a. to go alone.
    b. to hold hands and stick together.

6. Fulghum remembers the Styrofoam cups because
    a. he used to drink tea in them.
    b. he used to grow seeds in them.

7. Fulghum learned that goldfish, hamsters, and white mice
    a. all die—and so do we.
    b. eat a lot of food.

8. The word he learned from Dick-and-Jane books was
    a. look.
    b. stop.

SECTION C

9. He says some other things we learn in kindergarten are
    a. how to fool people and make a lot of money.
    b. ecology and the Golden Rule.

10. Fulghum thinks if we extrapolate any of these items and apply it to adults, it
    a. is still true.
    b. is not true.

11. Fulghum thinks it would be a better world if everyone
    a. ate only vegetables and prayed every day.
    b. had cookies and milk and lay down for a nap.

12. Fulghum thinks all governments should have a basic policy to
    a. put things back where they found them.
    b. change everything from the way it was before.

13. Fulghum thinks that countries around the world
    a. can learn a lot from the lessons of kindergarten.
    b. take naps every day.

14. When Fulghum says "it's best to hold hands and stick together," he means
    a. glue can keep your hands together.
    b. all people should help each other.

Listen again and check your answers. Share your answers with your partner. Then check your answers with the whole class and discuss any differences of opinion.

Listen Again

In this listening section, you will listen to the complete essay again, but this time there will be no pauses or narration between each section.

The sentences below contain information about the essay you just heard. In every sentence, there is some information that is not true about the essay. The information that is not true is <u>underlined</u>. The sentences are listed in the order that the information is heard on the tape. As you listen to the essay again, cross out the incorrect information and write the correct information above it.

Example: In this essay, Fulghum says he learned a lot of life lessons
Kindergarten
in <u>high school</u>.

Here are the sentences for you to change. Get ready to focus on the correct answer as you listen to the tape again.

1. Fulghum says that wisdom was not at the top of the graduate-school

   mountain, but there in the <u>classroom</u> at Sunday School.

2. Fulghum says to share <u>nothing</u>.

3. Fulghum says to <u>never</u> put things back where you found them.

4. Fulghum says that warm cookies and cold <u>soup</u> are good for you.

5. Fulghum says to take a <u>walk</u> every afternoon.

6. Fulghum says it's important to remember the Golden <u>Hen</u>.

3. Fulghum still thinks it's true that when you go out into the world, it's best to <u>wash</u> hands and stick together.

Listen to the tape again and check your answers with the rest of the class.

*C*lass Activities

What Do You Think?

Discuss with your class the answers to the following questions.

1. Why do you think this essay is so popular all around the world? Do you think you will share it with other people too? Why or why not?

2. What do you think Fulghum means when he advises people "to live a balanced life"? Do you think he is right?

3. Why do you think Fulghum says that "wonder" is such an important part of our lives? Do you agree or disagree with this idea?

4. Do you think this essay is only for children—or for adults too? Explain your answer.

5. The Golden Rule (treat other people the way you would like them to treat you) is a popular Western proverb. Do you have any similar proverb or expression in your culture? If so, share it with your class.

Personal Creations: A "Perfect" School Program

Throughout the world, schools and school programs come in many shapes and forms. Pretend that you are hired to create the *perfect* school program for either an elementary, high school, or college program in your country or in the United States. Think about the kinds of things you would want to include, such as the subjects you would teach, the amount of time for each subject each week or each day, how many students should be in each class, and what kind of instructional materials you would need. Do you think you would include teachers, or can you think of any other choice?

Take some notes on your ideas and when you feel ready, present your ideas orally to the class, to your group, or to your partner—or write about it and share your ideas on paper.

Reflections: Sharing Ideas Across the Cultures

Many years ago, the famous Greek philosopher Plato said that the education a person receives at a very early age will direct that person's whole life.

What do you think about this idea? Do you agree or disagree? Is this a popular or an unpopular idea in your culture? Share these thoughts with your partner.

Dictation

Listen and fill in the missing words.

These are the _____ I learned:

_____ everything.

Play _____ .

Don't _____ people.

Put things _____ where you _____ them.

_____ up your own _____ .

Don't _____ things that aren't _____ .

Say you're _____ when you _____ somebody.

_____ your hands _____ you eat.

_____ the toilet after you use it.

I learned that warm _____ and cold _____ are good for you.

I learned to _____ a _____ life— to _____ some and _____ some and _____ some and paint and dance and _____ and work some every day.

Speaking of Culture

New immigrants in the United States are often surprised by many things about U.S. education. One surprise is the large amount of independent thinking expected by the teachers. Teachers expect students to respond to questions with their own opinions and ideas, not just the opinions of the teacher or what is taught in books. Another common surprise is how much students participate in the classes, which is quite different from many other countries.

Read the following dialogue between Mark and José about the differences in their ideas about education. Mark was born in the United States, and José is a new immigrant from Guatemala. They are both in the same history class in high school and are now walking through the school on the way to class.

José: Mark, can I tell you about something that bothers me?

Mark: Sure.

José: I feel very strange about talking about my opinion in the history class. The teacher always says "What do you think about this?" and really, I don't know what to say. It's not like that in my country.

Mark: What was it like there?

José: Well, we came to class, copied and memorized what the teacher taught us, and nobody ever asked my opinion.

Mark: Well, you know, José. We all like to hear everyone's ideas—the students' and the teacher's. We learn a lot from each other, too. Sometimes a student mentions an idea we didn't think of before, and it helps us look at something in a new way.

José: It's hard for me to get used to this style of learning. I think it was an easier style in my country. Now I'm always worried that I don't have the "right" answer, when there are so many ways to think about one thing.

Mark: I guess it could be hard to get used to, but the teachers are trying to get us ready to live in American society. There are so many choices to make about our personal lives, such as choosing a career or where to live. There are also many decisions we need to make about the society, so we really need to develop skills to be able to think independently.

José: When you explain it like that, I understand it better. But it's still very difficult for me.

Now answer these questions.

1. Have you ever felt uncomfortable with the U.S. educational system or the system you live in now? Have you ever had the same feelings as José? Why or why not?

2. From what you've seen or heard, what do you think are the good parts of U.S. education, and what do you think are the bad parts?

3. How do schools in your country compare with schools in the United States?

Chapter 2

ALL THINGS ARE CONNECTED

The earth does not belong to man;
Man belongs to the earth.
Whatever he does to the earth,
He does to himself.
All things are connected—
Like the blood which unites one family—
All things are connected.

—*Chief Seattle*

*L*ook at the chapter title, the picture, and the quotation under the picture. What do you think this chapter is about? What does the picture tell you about the subject?

*C*hapter Preview

About Connections

Native Americans and other peoples have built their cultures and societies on the belief that nature, humans, plants, and animals all share the earth and are connected to one another. They believe that whatever is done to one part of the earth will be felt in all other parts of the earth. For example, if you throw a small stone into a lake, the waves it makes reach far in many directions. In the same way, if you cut down a tree you get the wood you need, but you also lose the shade that nearby animals and plants depend on.

Today, throughout many parts of the world, people of many countries are realizing what Native American societies have been teaching for centuries: people, the earth, and all living things are part of a chain of life. Each needs and depends on the other. Many people now realize that it is our responsibility to protect and save the earth and its environment in order for all life to continue. They believe we must all cooperate to find ways to stop polluting and destroying the earth's environment.

Interviewing Your Partner

Sit in groups of four students. Name each member of the group in the following way: Student A, Student B, Student C, and Student D. Students A and B should interview each other. Students C and D should interview each other.

Ask your partner the following interview questions and take notes on the answers.

1. What environmental problems around the world do you think are the most serious? Why?

   _____

   _____

2. Are there environmental problems in your country that people are trying to solve? How are they trying to solve them?

_____

_____

3. When you were growing up, did you feel connected to nature? In what ways?

_____

_____

4. Are there customs in your culture that show honor and respect for nature? What are they? How are they celebrated?

_____

_____

5. Do you think it is important for people always to feel a connection to the natural world around us? Why or why not? What ways can you suggest to help make this happen?

_____

_____

Reporting Your Information to the Group

Read over the notes you took about your partner. Then tell the group all about your partner's answers.

Writing the Group Report

(Optional)

Follow the instructions for this exercise in Chapter 1 (pages 5–6).

*V*ocabulary Preview

Words and Phrases

Before listening to the essay, let's preview some specific vocabulary words you will hear. In this section, each new vocabulary word is listed with its definition beside it. A sample sentence containing the new word or words follows the definition. In many cases, the sample sentences are taken directly from the essay you will hear. These sentences are marked with quotation marks.

WORDS or PHRASES	MEANING
1. unique	unusual
	(Example: "In the Solomon Islands, some villagers practice a **unique** form of logging.")
2. logging	the job of cutting down trees
	(Example: "**Logging** is an important industry in Washington State.")
3. to be felled	to have something fall down
	(Example: "If a tree is too large **to be felled** with an ax, the natives cut it down by yelling at it.")
4. ax	tool used to cut trees and wood
	(Example: "They took the **ax** and went to cut firewood.")
5. woodsmen	people who cut trees
	(Example: "**Woodsmen** with special powers creep up on a tree just at dawn and suddenly scream at it at the top of their lungs.")

WORDS or PHRASES	MEANING
6. to creep	to move slowly and quietly
	(Example: Her baby **creeps** slowly in front of the dog.)
7. "at the top of their lungs"	to yell as loudly as possible
	(Example: The kids saw the fire coming and yelled **at the top of their lungs** to get their parents out of the house.)
8. theory	idea that may be true
	(Example: "The **theory** is that hollering kills the trees.")
9. hollering	yelling
	(Example: The children are always **hollering** at the pets.)
10. to yell	to speak or shout loudly
	(Example: When you **yell** at people, it can hurt their feelings.)
11. "They may have a point."	They may be right
	(Example: "As for people, well, the Solomon Islanders **may have a point**.")
12. tend to	seem to; appear.
	(Example: "Yelling at living things does **tend to** kill the spirit in them.")

Vocabulary Quick-Check Review

Check your understanding of the new words and phrases introduced in this chapter by matching the words in column A with their closest definition in Column B.

Column A	Column B
1. ____ unique	a. yelling
2. ____ logging	b. they may be right
3. ____ to be felled	c. people who cut trees
4. ____ ax	d. to yell as loud as possible
5. ____ woodsmen	e. tool for cutting wood
6. ____ to creep	f. seems to
7. ____ to scream at the top of your lungs	g. an idea
8. ____ theory	h. to fall down
9. ____ hollering	i. to walk or crawl slowly
11. ____ tends to	j. cutting trees to get wood
10. ____ they have a point	k. unusual

*E*ssay Preview

Did you ever think that emotions were connected to making things die? In this chapter's essay, Fulghum tells us about the Solomon Islanders who yell at trees and make them fall down! He also shows us many ways that angry emotion is connected to destroying our spirits.

*F*ocused Listening

Look over the following questions before you listen to the tape. This will give you an idea of what information to focus on while listening to the essay the first time. The title and the section of each part you will listen to will be announced on the tape. Listen carefully to each listening section and then circle the correct answer for each question in that section.

What's This Story About?

1. In the Solomon Islands, if a tree can't be felled with an ax, the natives
   a. use an electric drill.
   b. yell at the tree.

2. At dawn, the woodsmen yell at the tree for
   a. 30 days.
   b. 38 days.

3. The theory is
   a. that hollering kills the tree.
   b. that the tree was already dead.

4. The villagers say
   a. hollering always works.
   b. hollering never works.

SECTION B

5. Mr. Fulghum says that he yells at
   a. his wife, the telephone, and the T.V.
   b. trees, insects, and flowers.

6. Fulghum says he shakes his fist at
   a. the radio.
   b. the sky.

7. Fulghum says the man next door yells at his
   a. car and stepladder.
   b. car and refrigerator.

8. Fulghum says we modern people yell most at
   a. machines and relatives.
   b. blue jeans and relatives.

SECTION C

9. Fulghum doesn't know
   a. what good yelling does.
   b. how to yell.

10. Fulghum says that when we yell at machines, they still
    a. work OK.
    b. just sit there.

11. Fulghum agrees with the Solomon Islanders and thinks
    a. yelling can kill the spirit of things.
    b. yelling at trees is a great idea.

12. Fulghum says that angry words
    a. never bother us.
    b. can break our hearts.

Listen again and check your answers. Share your answers with your partner. Then check your answers with the whole class and discuss any differences of opinion.

Listen Again

In this listening section, you will listen to the complete essay again, but this time there will be no pauses or narration in between each section.

The sentences below contain information about the essay you just heard. In every sentence, there is some information that is not true about the essay. The information that is not true is <u>underlined</u>. The sentences are listed in the order in which the information is heard on the tape. As you listen to the essay again, cross out the incorrect information and write the correct information above it.

Here are the sentences for you to change. Get ready to focus on the correct answer as you listen to the tape again.

1. Villagers in the <u>Hawaiian</u> Islands practice an unusual form of logging.

2. If a tree is too large to be cut with an ax, the villagers <u>sing to</u> it.

3. The tree falls down because the villagers kill the <u>wood</u> of the tree.

4. Fulghum says he yells at his <u>cat</u>.

5. The man next door to Fulghum yells at his <u>flowers</u> a lot.

6. Fulghum says that <u>birds</u> and relatives get most of the yelling.

7. Fulghum says that sticks and stones may break our <u>homes</u>.

8. Fulghum says that <u>love</u> will break our hearts.

Listen to the tape again and check your answers with the rest of the class.

*C*lass Activities

What Do You Think?

Discuss with your class the answers to the following questions.

1. Were you surprised that the Solomon Islanders say they they can yell at a tree and it falls down? Do you believe this story? Why or why not?

2. Mr. Fulghum gives a lot of examples of people yelling when they feel angry. Is yelling a common way to express anger in your culture? Why or why not? How do you express anger?

3. Mr. Fulghum gives examples of the way that negative words can hurt us. Do you think that the opposite is also true—that kind, helpful words can make us feel good? Why or why not? Can you think of any examples in your private life that show this?

4. Now that you have listened to this essay, why do you think the title is "All Things Are Connected"? Take another look at the illustration on the first page of the chapter for help with this answer.

Personal Creations: Letters to Congress

No matter what country we live in, we all share responsibility to keep the earth safe and clean. One way we can show our interest is to let government representatives know about our concerns and our opinions. One common way of doing this is to write letters to our local, state, and federal representatives.

Think about an environmental problem that most concerns you. Have you noticed anything in your present neighborhood or where you have lived in the past that is an environmental and health problem, such as dirty trash or polluted air or water?

Create and then write a short letter to a local government official expressing your concern about an environmental problem. Find out the address of the mayor or another representative of your local government and mail your letter to him or her. You may receive an answer that will suggest some things you can do to help solve the problem.

Here's a sample letter.

123 Elm St. Apt. 23
Chicago, IL 60611
June 10, 1994

Mayor Susan O'Brien
Homestead City Hall
456 Main St.
Homestead, IL 60012

Dear Mayor O'Brien:

I'm very worried about the dead fish I recently saw in a lake near my house. Some people told me that the fish died because of chemicals coming from a factory near the lake.

I am writing to you because I want to prevent more fish from dying and because I am worried about the effects these chemicals could have on people living near the lake. Please let me know what I can do to help and what your office can do to change the situation.

Thank you for your interest.

Sincerely,

Max Markham

Max Markham
ESL Student

Reflections: How Are Emotions Connected to Our Health?

In the 1970s, a famous American writer named Norman Cousins became very ill after an international trip. Doctors were not sure that Western medical techniques would be able to cure him. Mr. Cousins knew that he would have to be in the hospital for a long time, so he asked his family and friends to bring him videotapes of funny movies that he could watch while he was in the hospital. He watched these funny movies every day and laughed a lot. He noticed that while he was laughing, he didn't have as much pain as he had before. He started to think that happy emotions can cure his illness.

Doctors were very surprised when they saw Mr. Cousins's health improve a lot. Although he had been taking several forms of medication before he began his "laugh therapy," he had not improved much. They all agreed that that laughing every day helped Mr. Cousins get well again. You can read more about Mr. Cousins's experiences in his book *Anatomy of an Illness*..

Now answer these questions.

1. Are you surprised that Mr. Cousins's health improved from laughing? Why or why not? Have you ever heard anything like this before?

2. In your culture, are emotions thought to be an important part of good health? When a doctor in your culture advises patients about their health, does he or she talk about their happy or unhappy feelings, in addition to giving medicine? Please explain.

3. Mr. Cousins's story tells about the benefit of good emotions on a person's health. Do you think that unhappy emotions can create problems for a person's health? Why or why not? Have you had any personal experience dealing with the effect of emotions on health?

4. Why do you think this story about Mr. Cousins was included in a chapter of this book called "All Things Are Connected"?

Dictation

Listen and fill in the missing words.

In the Solomon Islands in the South Pacific, some
villagers practice a _____ form of _____ .
If a tree is too large to be _____ with an _____ ,
the natives cut it down by _____ at it. _____ with
special powers _____ up on a tree just at dawn and
suddenly _____ at it at the top of their _____ .
They continue this for _____ days. And the tree dies
and _____ _____ . The theory is that the _____ kills
the spirit of the tree. _____ to the villagers,
it always works.

Speaking of Culture

How we express our emotions depends very much on the way we grew
up in our culture. In this chapter's essay, "All Things Are Connected,"
Fulghum uses the example of "yelling" as a way some people express
anger. Because the United States includes many cultures, it is not
possible to describe just one way that Americans show anger. Sometimes
anger is openly expressed, and sometimes it is never openly expressed.
It will always depend on the people and the situations.

In the U.S. workplace, however, there are more common expectations of
expressing anger or unhappiness about something that happened on the
job, either with co-workers or the boss. Most U.S. employers think
workers have the right to express their opinions—including anger—but
they are expected to express them in a calm and controlled way, such as
setting up an appointment to discuss the problem. Some newcomers to
the United States find this freedom and openness very surprising.

Robert and Ali, a new immigrant from Africa, both work in the same
auto repair shop. It's Friday, and they both go to the front office to get
their weekly checks at the same time. Robert sees that when Ali opens
his check, he looks very upset.

Robert: Ali, is something wrong?

Ali: Yes, I'm very angry at the boss.

Robert: What happened?

Ali: The boss promised me a raise this week, but this check is for the same amount of money as last week.

Robert: Maybe there was some kind of mistake.

Ali: I think he lied to me, but I can't do anything about it. He's the boss.

Robert: How about asking him about the check?

Ali: What?

Robert: Talk to the boss about the check. Maybe there was a mistake somewhere.

Ali: Are you sure? Maybe he will want to fire me if I ask him about this.

Robert: If the boss told you about a raise and it's not on the check, you have a right to ask him about it.

Ali: OK. I'm really mad. I'll go see him now.

Robert: It's really better if you calm down first. Then leave the boss a note that you'd like to talk to him when he gets a chance.

Ali: OK. I'll follow your advice.

Robert: Good luck!

Next Tuesday Robert and Ali meet during the break time.

Ali: Hi, Robert. I was looking for you.

Robert: Why?

Ali: I want to thank you for your advice about talking to the boss.

Robert: What happened?

Ali: He talked to me this morning, and there <u>was</u> a mistake. He forgot to tell the accountant to add the raise to my salary check. He told me I will have a raise for this week and next week on next Friday's check.

Robert: Congratulations!

Ali: Well, I really have to thank you for your advice. Sometimes things seem very strange to me about life here. It's nice to have a good friend like you!

Now answer these questions.

1   Are you surprised by the advice Robert gave Ali? Why or why not?

2.   If you were Ali and saw that the raise the boss had promised was not included in the check, what would you do? In the United States? In your country?

3.   Do you think talking to the boss when you have a problem at work is an easy thing for you to do or a difficult thing? Explain.

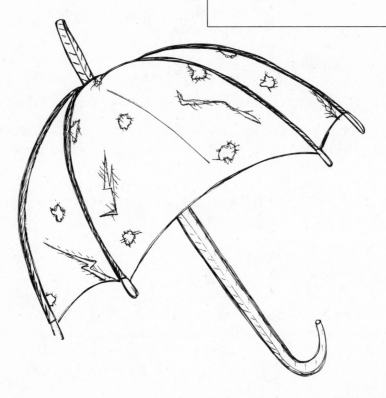

One day, two men from the town of Chelm (a village very far away) went for a walk. Suddenly it began to rain. "Quick," said one man. "Open your umbrella!" "Sorry. It won't help," said the other man. "My umbrella is full of holes." "Then why did you bring an umbrella?" asked the first man. "I didn't think it would rain!!!!" the other man answered.

—*William Novak, Moshe Waldoks*
The Big Book of Jewish Humor

*L*ook at the chapter title, the picture, and the short story below the picture. What do you think this chapter is about? What does the picture tell you about the subject?

*C*hapter Preview

About Using Stories for Lessons

Since ancient times, people have used stories to teach lessons to guide and encourage people in their everyday life. For example, great religious leaders such as Jesus, Mohammed, and Buddha all used stories to teach their beliefs about religion and human experiences. Today many of these same stories from over a thousand years ago are still remembered and taught from generation to generation for their universal messages.

Stories with serious purposes can also make us laugh. In some cultures, clowns and comedians are admired for being able to help us laugh at ourselves. The stories permit us to see difficult situations in a less serious way. Sometimes adding humor helps us live with and understand a problem better and keeps us hopeful. There can be great lessons in comedy, and many people believe that there is a bit of truth in every funny story.

Interviewing Your Partner

Sit in groups of four students. Name each member of the group in the following way: Student A, Student B, Student C, and Student D. Students A and B should interview each other. Students C and D should interview each other.

Ask your partner the following interview questions and take notes on the answers.

1. Is it popular in your culture to use stories to teach lessons? If "yes," are these stories told for adults or both children and adults?

2. When you were a child, did anyone tell you stories? Who was this person? What were the stories about?

3. Are clowns and comedians admired in your culture? Why or why not?

4. Do you agree or disagree that there is a bit of truth in every funny story?

Reporting Your Information to the Group

Read over the notes you took about your partner. Then tell the group all about your partner's answers.

Telling or Writing the Group Report

(Optional)

Follow the directions for this exercise in Chapter 1 (pages 5–6).

$\mathcal{V}$ocabulary Preview

Words and Phrases

Before listening to the essay, let's preview some specific vocabulary words you will hear. In this section, each new vocabulary word is listed with its definition beside it, followed by a sample sentence containing the new word or words. If the sample sentence is taken directly from the essay you will hear, the sentence is marked with quotation marks.

WORDS or PHRASES	MEANING
1. troubled	feeling upset about a problem (Example: "A **troubled** man paid a visit to his rabbi.")
2. wise	smart (Example: "Please say something **wise**, Rabbi.")
3. to wring his hands	holding and twisting his hands together in a nervous way (Example: "Rabbi," said he, **wringing his hands**, "I am a failure.")
4. a failure	a person who is never successful (Example: "I am **a failure**. More than half the time I do not succeed in doing what I must do.")

WORDS or PHRASES	MEANING
5. pondering	thinking a lot about something (Example: "After much **pondering**, the rabbi spoke.")
6. wisdom	smart ideas or smart advice (Example: "Ah, my son. I give you this **wisdom**.")
7. an almanac	a book that is published every year that contains facts and information about general topics (Example: "He looked in the **almanac** to find the average temperature in Chicago for the month of June.")
8. batting average	a decimal number (examples: .400, .325, and .275) telling how often a baseball player gets a hit (Example: "Now this is what he found: The listing of the lifetime **batting averages** of all the greatest baseball players.")
9. slugger	a slang word referring to a baseball player who can hit the ball a long distance (Example: "Ty Cobb, the greatest **slugger** of all, had a surprising batting average.")
10. a "hit"	when the hitter hits the baseball and reaches a base before the other team throws the ball to that base (Example: "He got **a hit** once out of every three times it was his turn to hit the ball.")

11. theology   the study of God and religions

                 (Example: "**Theology** is amazing.")

12. abound   something that is found in many places

                 (Example: "Holy books **abound**.")

Vocabulary Quick-Check Review

Check your understanding of the new words and phrases introduced in this chapter by matching the words in column A with their closest definition in Column B.

Column A	Column B
1. ____ slugger	a. upset about something
2. ____ abound	b. someone who doesn't succeed
3. ____ an almanac	c. to be smart
4. ____ a failure	d. thinking
5. ____ batting average	e. study of religions
6. ____ troubled	f. to hold and twist hands
7. ____ pondering	g. smart advice
8. ____ wisdom	h. book of facts
9. ____ a "hit"	i. when a hitter runs to first base before the other team throws the ball to the base
10. ____ theology	j. something that is all over
11. ____ to be wise	k. a hitter who can hit the ball very far
12. ____ to wring one's hands	l. a number telling how successful a hitter is

$\mathcal{E}$ssay Preview

In this chapter's essay, "What's So Funny?," a man who is feeling very upset about his problems goes to a rabbi (a Jewish religious leader and teacher) for advice. The rabbi gives the man advice by telling him to find out the lifetime baseball average of a very famous baseball player named Ty Cobb and then return to the rabbi with the information. With this very funny advice, the rabbi teaches the man an important lesson. What kinds of lessons do you think can be learned from baseball scores?

In order to help you understand this essay better, here's a brief introduction to the game of baseball:

WHAT'S BASEBALL?

Baseball is a very popular team game in the United States, Canada, and other places in the world. There are nine people on each team. The main goal of the game is for each team to make as many runs (points) as possible. Whichever team has the most runs wins the game.

HOW DOES A PLAYER GET A RUN?

Most players get a few chances in each game to try to get a run. When it's a player's turn, he or she stands in front of a triangle-shaped marker, home plate. (Home plate is one of four markers; the other three are first base, second base, and third base.) A player from the other team (the pitcher) throws a ball to the player on the first team, who tries to hit the ball with a bat—a long wooden stick. If this player (the batter or hitter) hits the ball, it can be good news or bad news.

HOW CAN IT BE BAD NEWS?

If a player from the opposite team (a fielder) catches the ball before it bounces, then the batter doesn't get any more chances to hit the ball in that turn.

HOW CAN IT BE GOOD NEWS?

If the batter hits the ball and the ball bounces, the fielder on the opposite team must get the ball to the base before the batter gets there. If the batter reaches the base before the fielder gets the ball to the base, then it's called a "hit." When the batter can touch all four bases before he or she is caught, a run is made for the team. The hitter can also get a run if he or she hits the ball so far that no fielder can catch it (it may go out of the stadium or into the crowd).

WHAT'S A BATTING AVERAGE?

A batting average is each player's personal score of how often he or she has made a hit. If a batter got a hit every time he or she got a turn, the hitter's batting average would be .1000. If the batter got a hit half of the times he or she got a turn, the batting average would be .500. If the batter got a hit one time every four times he or she had a turn, the batting average would be .250.

What would a player's batting average be if he or she made one hit every five times the person batted?

$\mathcal{F}$ocused Listening

Look over the following questions before you listen to the tape. This will give you an idea of what information to focus on while listening to the essay the first time. The title and the section of each part you will listen to will be announced on the tape. Listen carefully to each listening section, and then circle the correct answer for each question in that section.

What's This Story About?

SECTION A

1. A troubled man went to the rabbi
    a. for help.
    b. to have dinner.

2. The man was upset because
    a. he felt he was a failure.
    b. he had to bring his car to be repaired.

3. To get peace of mind, the rabbi told the man to
    a. look in the 1970 *New York Times Almanac*.
    b. look in the 1980 *New York Times Almanac*.

4. The man went away and
    a. didn't do it.
    b. did do it.

SECTION B

5. The almanac contained
   a. the lifetime batting average of Ty Cobb.
   b. the lifetime basketball scores of Ty Cobb.

6. Ty Cobb's average was
   a. .367.
   b. .467.

7. Babe Ruth's lifetime batting average
   a. was more than Ty Cobb's.
   b. was less than Ty Cobb's.

SECTION C

8. When the man went back to the rabbi, he wanted the rabbi
   a. to explain the meaning of the scores.
   b. to give the man another question.

9. Ty Cobb's batting average showed that every three times he tried to hit the ball in a baseball game,
   a. he only hit it two times.
   b. he only hit it one time.

10. The rabbi wanted to show the man
    a. that Ty Cobb liked baseball.
    b. that a famous star like Ty Cobb sometimes didn't succeed.

SECTION D

11. When the man finally understood the rabbi's lesson,
    a. he felt better.
    b. he wanted to learn how to play baseball.

12. Fulghum says, "Theology is amazing, and holy books abound." This means:
    a. He likes to read amazing things.
    b. You can learn many surprising lessons in unusual books.

Listen again and check your answers. Share your answers with your partner. Then check your answers with the whole class and discuss any differences of opinion.

Listen Again

In this section, you will listen to the complete essay again, but this time there will be no pauses or narration in between each section.

The sentences below contain information about the essay you just heard. In every sentence, there is some information that is not true about the essay. The information that is not true is <u>underlined</u>. The sentences are listed in the order that the information is heard on the tape. As you listen to the essay again, cross out the incorrect information and write the correct information above it.

Here are the sentences for you to change. Get ready to focus on the correct answer as you listen to the tape again.

1. A <u>happy</u> man went to see his rabbi.

2. He told the rabbi he was a <u>success</u>.

3. He said to the rabbi, "Rabbi, please say something <u>funny</u>."

4. The rabbi told him to look in the *New York Times* <u>phone book</u>.

5. The man found the lifetime batting averages for famous <u>football</u> players.

6. He found the scores for a man called <u>Magic Johnson</u>.

7. This man had a batting average of <u>.591</u>.

8. Fulghum says that theology is <u>boring</u>.

Listen to the tape again and check your answers with the rest of the class.

Class Activities

What Do You Think?

Discuss with your class the answers to the following questions.

1. What do you think about the way the rabbi taught a lesson to the troubled man? Do you think the rabbi was wise? Why or why not?

2. If someone in your culture needed advice, where would he or she go? In your culture, are there any particular religious or spiritual leaders or other advisers who help people with their problems? Who are they? Have you ever visited one of these people for a problem you were having? If yes, what happened?

3. The problem of the troubled man in the story is feeling successful. Each society has a different idea about what success is. In your culture, what are the characteristics of a successful person?

4. Pretend that you have a close friend who comes to you for advice. This person feels like a failure. He or she thinks success is not possible for him or her. What advice would you give?

Dictation

Listen and fill in the missing words.

After much _____ , the Rabbi spoke as follows: "Ah, my son, I give you this _____ : Go and look on page 930 of *The New York Times* _____ for the year 1970, and you will find _____ _____ _____ maybe."

"Ah," said the man, and he went away and did that _____ .

Now this is what he _____ : The listing of the lifetime _____ _____ of all the greatest baseball players.

Personal Creations: Tell Your Favorite Story

In this chapter, Mr. Fulghum shared a favorite story of his about a rabbi and Ty Cobb. Think about a story that you know that teaches a lesson about everyday problems, or create a story, true or not true. In student groups or in front of the class, tell your story! After the group or class has listened to all the stories, choose one that you really like and write a few sentences describing it.

Reflections: What Do You Think Is Funny?

A RETURN TO CHELM

The story is told that in the town of Chelm, there are both wise people and foolish people. Of course, everyone believes that he or she is one of the wise ones. The people of Chelm are always interested in solving problems and always seem to have a reason for all their solutions. Let's listen to one of their conversations.

Wise man 1:	I have been looking for an answer to this problem for a long time. Which do you think is more important—the sun or the moon?
Wise man 2:	Oh, that is an easy question to answer. The moon is more important.
Wise man 1:	Why?
Wise man 2:	At night the moon is very important because it gives us light when it is very dark. But in the day it is already light, so why do we need the sun?

Well, what do you think?

Go back to the Chelm story and the picture on the first page of this chapter. Do you notice anything the same or different about these two stories? What do you notice? Do you think there is a bit of truth in either or both of these stories?

Maybe you will be surprised to learn that there really is a town called Chelm in Poland, but as is the case with many old folktales, no one is quite sure why this town became so popular for its fools.

Chelm stories were very popular throughout Eastern Europe, but stories about towns of fools who taught unusual lessons were also popular in England and ancient Greece.

Each culture has its own folktales and humorous traditions. And the things we may think are funny in our society and culture may not be considered funny in other cultures. For example, in the United States, there are jokes about many subjects—politics, sports, religion, and the American lifestyle. These topics, however, may not be used for jokes in other societies.

Do you remember any funny folktales from your culture you would like to share with the class? In your culture, which topics are most frequently used for humor? Are there any topics that are never talked about in humorous ways? Which topics are they?

Speaking of Culture

The United States is a society that openly uses comedy to make us laugh at ourselves as individuals. Americans frequently use comedy to show political leaders in humorous ways. Many newcomers to the United States are used to a more closed society where jokes are not made publicly about their leaders.

Here's a conversation between Natalia, a new immigrant from Eastern Europe, and her co-worker Anna.

Natalia: Anna, you know I saw a comedy show last night on TV. One funny man was pretending to be the president.

Anna: Did you like it?

Natalia: Well, it surprised me.

Anna: Because it was so funny?

Natalia: No, not really. I was surprised because in my country we don't make jokes about our political leaders publicly.

Anna: Oh. Well, here in the United States, this openness is a big part of the way we think democracy should work. We believe that it's the president's job to serve and represent the people, but at the same time we view him as an American just like the rest of us. We honor and respect him as our leader, and making jokes about him doesn't mean we don't respect him.

Natalia: I think these jokes make the president look very small in front of the rest of the world.

Anna: Natalia, our Constitution guarantees freedom of speech for every American. This also includes making jokes about our political leaders. Sometimes being able to express our disagreements with our leaders in a funny way can help change the way the leaders do things.

Natalia: Was it always like this in the United States?

Anna: Yes. From our earliest years as a country, newspapers and magazines always showed our leaders in both good and bad ways. Today, because we have television, there are more public ways to see our leaders so there are more public ways to show our opinions about them, good or bad.

Natalia: Thanks for the information, but it still seems very strange to me.

Now answer these questions.

1. Natalia said that she feels strange about watching jokes about U.S. political leaders on TV. How do you feel about this? Do you think it's a good idea? Why or why not?

2. Is it common or uncommon in your country to make jokes publicly about your political leaders? Explain.

3. If you were the director of a TV comedy show, would you include jokes about U.S. political leaders? Why or why not? What other subjects do you think you would include in your comedy show?

Chapter 4

NOT QUITE YET

Time is the stream I go fishing in.

—*H. D. Thoreau,*
adapted from Walden

Look at the chapter title, the picture, and the quotation above the picture. What do you think this chapter is about? What does the picture tell you about the subject?

*C*hapter Preview

About Time

The way a society or culture thinks about time can be seen in the way its people use language. The United States is well known for its very direct, active "do-it-now" lifestyle. Americans also use language in a very direct way, preferring to ask exact questions they expect to be answered with the direct "yes" or "no." Americans expect people to answer questions about time with exact answers, such as "The meeting's at two o'clock" or "We're having a party next Saturday at 8 P.M."

On the other hand, in many other cultures language reflects ancient beliefs and philosophies that time is a fairly unmeasurable, indirect thing. When people in these societies ask questions, they prefer to answer with less exact answers—such as "probably" or "maybe" rather than "yes" or "no." When using language to answer questions about time, the people also prefer indirect answers—such as "soon" or "later," giving the impression of things "possibly" happening often without exact beginnings or endings.

Interviewing Your Partner

Sit in groups of four students. Name each member of the group in the following way: Student A, Student B, Student C, and Student D. Students A and B should interview each other. Students C and D should interview each other.

Ask your partner the following interview questions and take notes on the answers.

1. Do you think the custom in your culture is to answer questions in a direct or indirect way? Give some examples of how you might answer some usual questions about yourself or an event that show a direct or indirect answer.

_____

_____

2. What are the questions most commonly asked in your culture when you meet someone new?

_____

_____

3. In your culture, are any questions considered impolite and never asked? If yes, what are they?

_____

_____

4. In your culture, are children encouraged to ask a lot of questions? Why or why not?

_____

_____

5. Can you think of any other ways the ideas of time are reflected in your culture? How important is it to be on time? Is relaxing and not doing things thought of as better than always doing things ? Explain.

_____

_____

Reporting Your Information to the Group

Read over the notes you took about your partner. Then tell the group all about your partner's answers.

Telling or Writing the Group Report

(Optional)

Follow the directions for this exercise in Chapter 1 (pages 5–6).

$\mathcal{V}$ocabulary Preview

Words and Phrases

Before listening to the essay, let's preview some specific vocabulary words you will hear. In this section, each new vocabulary word is listed with its definition beside it, followed by a sample sentence containing the new word or words. If the sample sentence is taken directly from the essay you will hear, the sentence is marked with quotation marks.

WORDS or PHRASES	MEANING
1. to be observed	to be seen or noted
	(Example: "Americans, it **is observed**, prefer definite answers.")
2. yea-yea and nay-nay	yes and no
	(Example: "Let your **yea-yea** be your **yea-yea** and your **nay-nay** be your **nay-nay**.")
3. gray	a color used to describe an opinion in between "yes" and "no"
	(Example: "No **grays**, please.")
4. to wire around	to replace
	(Example: "In Indonesia, there is a word in common use which nicely **wires around** the need for black and white.") (**Note:** The colors black and white are used when describing a definite "yes" and a definite "no.")
5. continuing possibility	the chance that something might happen at any time
	(Example: "Belum is a lovely word implying **continuing possibility**.")
6. cynical	sarcastic, thinking the worst of people
	(Example: "It is considered both impolite and **cynical** to say 'no' outright [at the beginning].")
7. the realm of what might be	something that may come true
	(Example: "Not yes or no, but within **the realm of what might be**.")

WORDS or PHRASES	MEANING
8. soft edges	feelings that anything is possible
	(Example: "**Soft edges** are welcome in this bus ride of human adventure.")
9. happily ever after	happy for the rest of your life
	(Example: "Will we live **happily ever after**?")

Vocabulary Quick-Check Review

Check your understanding of the new words and phrases introduced in this chapter by matching the words in column A with their closest definition in Column B.

Column A

1. _____ gray
2. _____ yea-yea or nay-nay
3. _____ to wire around
4. _____ continuing possibility
5. _____ cynical
6. _____ realm of what might be
7. _____ soft edges
8. _____ happily ever after

9. _____ to be observed

Column B

a. something that might come true

b. something that's always possible

c. happy for the rest of your life

d. sarcastic

e. feelings that anything is possible

f. to replace

g. to be seen

h. a color that describes an opinion between yes and no

i. yes or no

$\mathcal{E}$ssay Preview

In this chapter's essay Fulghum talks about how different cultures, particularly Indonesia, express ideas about time when people in that culture answer questions. According to Fulghum, people in Indonesia frequently use a popular word, *belum*, meaning "not quite yet" to answer questions. How do you think the Indonesians answer the question "Do you speak English?" Listen and find out.

*F*ocused Listening

Look over the following questions before you listen to the tape. This will give you an idea of what information to focus on while listening to the essay the first time. The title and the section of each part you will listen to will be announced on the tape. Listen carefully to each listening section, then circle the correct answer for each question in that section.

What's This Story About?

SECTION A

1. Americans prefer
   a. definite answers.
   b. gray answers.

2. The word *belum* is used in
   a. South Africa.
   b. Indonesia.

3. The word *belum* means
   a. I'm all wet.
   b. not quite yet.

4. Indonesians use the word *belum* because
   a. it is not polite to answer "no."
   b. it's a funny word.

5. How do the people in Indonesia answer the questions "Do you speak English" and "Is the taxi on fire?"
   a. yes.
   b. *belum*.

SECTION B

6. "Maybe" and "possibly" mean
   a. definitely "yes."
   b. within the realm of what might be.

7. Fulghum says soft edges are welcome
   a. in white-water adventures.
   b. in this bus ride of human adventure.

8. Fulghum
   a. is sure that this is the best of all possible worlds.
   b. thinks this might be the best of all possible worlds.

9. Fulghum asks:
   a. Is the world coming to an end?
   b. When will the world end?

10. Fulghum thinks
    a. we can never do without the weapons of war.
    b. we might be able to do without the weapons of war.

Listen again and check your answers. Share your answers with your partner. Then check your answers with the whole class and discuss any differences of opinion.

Listen Again

In this listening section, you will listen to the complete essay again, but this time there will be no pauses or narration between each section.

The sentences below contain information about the essay you just heard. In every sentence, there is some information that is not true about the essay. The information that is not true is <u>underlined</u>. The sentences are listed in the order that the information is heard on the tape. As you listen to the essay again, cross out the incorrect information and write the correct information above it.

Here are the sentences for you to change. Get ready to focus on the correct answer as you listen to the tape again.

1. Fulghum says <u>Japanese</u> people prefer definite answers.

2. Fulghum says, "Let your yea-yea be your <u>nay-nay</u>."

3. *Belum* is a word used in <u>Canada</u>.

4. *Belum* is a word that means <u>ending</u> possibilities.

5. It is considered <u>polite</u> to say "no" outright.

6. Fulghum says that soft edges are considered <u>unwelcome</u> in the "bus ride of adventure."

7. Fulghum asks if this is the <u>worst</u> of all possible worlds.

8. Fulghum asks if we can do without the <u>music</u> of war.

Listen to the tape again and check your answers with the rest of the class.

*C*lass Activities

What Do You Think?

Discuss with your class the answers to the following questions.

1. Are you surprised that the word *belum* has so many meanings? Is there a word in your language that is similar to the word *belum*?

2. How would you answer the question "Do you speak English?"

3. Have you had any experiences from personal conversations, movies, or TV which have shown Americans using very direct language? Tell these experiences to the class.

4. What do you think Fulghum means when he says "soft edges" or indirect answers are welcome in this bus ride of human adventure?

5. Why do you think Fulghum thinks that the word *belum* is a good answer for the question "Can we do without the weapons of war"?

Personal Creations: Questionnaires

It is popular in the United States to write questionnaires, forms with questions to ask people their opinions. As a class—or individually—create a questionnaire with eight questions. Choose five questions that Fulghum uses in this essay and then write three additional questions of your own.

Example: 1. Do you speak English?
                 2. Is this the best of all possible worlds?
                 3. Which culture cooks the tastiest food?

Go around the room with your questionnaire and ask three students the questions on your questionnaire. Take notes on the answers. Then return to your seat with the completed questionnaires and share the answers with your classmates.

How many students answered most of the questions with direct answers? How many students answered questions indirectly? Which questions got the most direct answers? Which questions got the most indirect answers?

Reflections: About Time

A few years ago, an interesting story about time was in the newspaper. It was about a group of miners (people who work in a mine) caught in an underground mine in Germany. When they saw that they could not get out, they knew there was only enough air to keep them alive for a few hours. Only one man was wearing a watch. He wanted to keep all the men hopeful and alive while they waited for a rescue. The men asked the man with the watch to announce the time every hour, but instead he announced it every two hours and told them it was only one hour that had passed. The other men thought they were underground for only a few hours, but it was actually six days before they were rescued. All the men were alive except one—the man who had the watch.

Now answer these questions.

1. Why do you think the man with the watch died and the other men didn't?

2. What ideas does this story give you about the idea of time?

3. What's your opinion of the actions of the man with the watch?

4. Do you think you might do the same thing as the man with the watch? Why or why not?

5. In your culture, would the man with the watch be a hero? Why or why not?

Dictation

Listen and fill in the missing words.

In Indonesia, however, there is a word in common _____
that nicely _____ around the need for black and
white. _____ is the word and it means "_____
_____ _____ ." A lovely word implying
continuing _____ . "Do you speak _____ ?"
"*Belum.*" Not quite yet. "Do you _____ any
_____ ?" "*Belum.*" "Do you know the
_____ of life?" "*Belum.*" It is considered
both _____ and _____ to say "No" outright
to important questions. This leads to some funny _____ .
"Is the _____ on fire?" "*Belum.*" _____ _____ _____ .

Speaking of Culture

Since Americans are famous for their direct questions and direct answers,
many newcomers to the United States are surprised to learn that there
are several subjects of conversation that Americans speak about very
indirectly. The most common examples of these subjects are how much
money someone makes on a job and the exact price someone pays for
something (usually larger items like a house or a car). Questions about
these subjects are discussed in conversation, but in a very indirect way.
Here's an example.

Marta, a student from Eastern Europe, has been in the United States for
six months. She has become friendly with her next door, American-born
neighbor, Judi. When they see each other they always say "hello" and
talk for a few minutes. Today Judi had a day off from her job, and Marta
began a conversation with her.

Marta: Hi, Judi.

Judi: Hi, Marta. How are you today?

Marta: I'm fine. I'm going to go to my English class in a few minutes.

Judi: That's nice. I've got a day off today, and I feel like being very lazy.

Marta: Don't you like your job?

Judi: Sure, I like it, but it's nice to have some free time. I'm always very busy at work.

Marta: It's nice you like your job. How much money do you make?

Judi: Excuse me?

Marta: (Repeats the same question.) How much money do you make?

Judi: (She feels very embarrassed and surprised to be asked that question.) Well, it's a good salary. I've worked there for five years already.

Marta: (She is thinking, "What's a good salary?") Oh. Well, I saw your husband driving a different car today. Is it new?

Judi: It's three years old.

Marta: What did you pay for it?

Judi: (Again feels embarrassed but is beginning to realize that Marta does not realize she is asking impolite questions.) Marta, it's really impolite here to ask direct questions about prices or salaries. It's more polite to ask indirect questions like "How's the salary?" if you ask about a job, and "Did you get a good price?" when you ask about something someone bought. Sometimes people will answer directly, and sometimes they will answer indirectly. It really depends on the person.

Marta: Thanks for telling me. I didn't mean to be impolite.

Judi: That's OK. There's a lot to learn in a new country!

Now answer these questions.

1. Are you surprised about Judi's answers to Marta's questions? Why or why not?

2. Is it common in your culture to ask questions about salary and prices in a direct or indirect way? Give examples to the class to show this.

3. Are there things in your culture that are impolite to ask about? Share these questions with the class. Compare the different impolite questions in different cultures. Are there similarities? Differences?

Chapter 5

GOOD NEWS

It's early morning, and a phone rings in Murray's apartment. Murray, a man who enjoys jokes and also hates bad news, answers the phone and immediately asks:

Hello? Is this somebody calling with good news or money?

It's not?

I'm sorry. Good-bye.

Then Murray hangs up the phone and goes back to sleep.

—Herb Gardner
adapted from the play *A Thousand Clowns*

*L*ook at the chapter title, the picture, and the short conversation below the picture. What do you think this chapter is about? What do the picture and conversation tell you about the subject?

*C*hapter Preview

About Good News

Although we may not realize it, learning about bad news in our private life or even in other parts of the world can affect our health and the way we feel. A recent article in *Natural Health* magazine told the story of a very healthy young man who went to the doctor because he couldn't sleep at night. The doctor did a lot of tests, but couldn't find any problem with the man. The doctor asked the man to describe his daily life in detail, hoping to find out if his personal life or job might be causing this problem. The man said one interesting thing. He told the doctor that he always watches world news on TV right before he goes to bed. The doctor advised him to change this and to watch the news at another time.

What do you think happened? After the man stopped watching the news before bed, he had no more problem falling asleep!

Even if we don't have a health problem like the man in the magazine article, all of us know that we feel better when we hear good news rather than bad news. Our spirits are lifted when we hear or see stories about difficult problems that were solved or about people helping other people. Most of us want to believe that there is more good than bad in ourselves and in the people around us.

Interviewing Your Partner

Sit in groups of four students. Name each member of the group in the following way: Student A, Student B, Student C, and Student D. Students A and B should interview each other. Students C and D should interview each other.

Ask your partner the following interview questions and take notes on the answers.

1. In your opinion, what things on the world news could have made the man so upset he couldn't sleep? Have you ever had a similar experience? Describe the situation to your partner.

   _____

   _____

2. What good news have you heard about lately? Use examples from your own life or the rest of the world.

   _____

   _____

3. How do you find out about world news? Do you read a newspaper or a magazine, or watch TV? What language do you use to read or listen to the news?

   _____

   _____

4. Go back to the conversation on the first page of this chapter. What did you think about the man's conversation? How do you think he was feeling that day? Have you ever had similar feelings about answering the phone? Describe the situation.

   _____

   _____

5. Do you agree or disagree with the idea that there is more good then bad in most people? What experiences have given you this opinion?

   _____

   _____

Reporting Your Information to the Group

Read over the notes you took about your partner. Then tell the group all about your partner's answers.

Telling or Writing the Group Report

(Optional)

Follow the instructions for this exercise in Chapter 1 (pages 5–6).

$\mathcal{V}$ocabulary Preview

Words and Phrases

Before listening to the essay, let's preview some specific vocabulary words you will hear. In this section, each new vocabulary word is listed with its definition beside it, followed by a sample sentence containing the new word or words. If the sample sentence is taken directly from the essay you will hear, the sentence is marked with quotation marks.

WORDS or PHRASES	MEANING
1. to rip you off	to cheat you
	(Example: "They're all out **to rip you off**, right?")
2. It ain't necessarily so.	It's not always like that.
	(Example: You might think everyone wants to cheat you, but **it ain't necessarily so**.)
3. to pose as a well-to-do foreigner	to pretend to be a rich person from another country
	(Example: "Bill **posed as a well-to-do foreigner** with little knowledge of English.")
4. to predict	to say what you expect to happen in the future
	(Example: She looked at his hand and **predicted** he would have a long life.)
5. to take advantage of someone	to use someone for your own benefit or profit
	(Example: "His friends predicted in advance that most would **take advantage of** him in some way.")

WORDS or PHRASES	MEANING
6. an irony	the opposite of what you expect (Example: "The greatest **irony** of all was that several drivers warned him that New York City was full of crooks and to be careful.")
7. corruption	actions that are caused by not being honest (Example: "You will continue to read stories of crookedness and **corruption**.")
8. on the take	describing taking money for doing something illegal (Example: Joe was caught being **on the take** after his boss discovered that he was taking money from people without tickets and letting them into the baseball stadium.)
9. evidence	proof (Example: The fingerprints on the gun were the **evidence** that showed he was the killer.)
10. a survey	questions people are asked about their opinions on a topic (Example: The director took a transportation **survey** of the workers and found out that most of them took public transportation to work.)
11. a Gallup survey	a survey prepared by one of the most popular U.S. public survey companies (Example: "A recent **survey by Gallup** indicates that 70 percent of the people believe that most people can be trusted most of the time.")

Vocabulary Quick-Check Review

Check your understanding of the new words and phrases introduced in this chapter by matching the words in column A with their closest definition in Column B.

Column A	Column B
1. ____ to rip you off	a. describing someone who takes money for illegal actions
2. ____ It ain't necessarily so.	b. to pretend to be a rich visitor
3. ____ theory	c. proof
4. ____ to pose as a well-to-do foreigner	d. to use someone for your own benefit
5. ____ to predict	e. a popular U.S. survey
6. ____ a survey	f. to say what will happen in the future
7. ____ irony	g. dishonest actions
8. ____ corruption	h. it's not always true
9. ____ on the take	i. to cheat you
10. ____ evidence	j. questions about your opinion
11. ____ Gallup	k. the opposite of what you expect
12. ____ to take advantage of someone	l. idea

*E*ssay Preview

In this chapter's essay, Fulghum talks about people's opinions about being able to trust other people. He tells the story of Steve Brill, a man in New York City who wanted to see how many taxi drivers would try to cheat him if they thought he was a foreign visitor and didn't speak English. All of Steve's friends believed that all taxi drivers would try to cheat him. But Steve had some very surprising news about his taxicab experiences. How many taxicab drivers do you think tried to cheat him?

$\mathcal{F}$ocused Listening

Look over the following questions before you listen to the tape. This will give you an idea of what information to focus on while listening to the essay the first time. The title and the section of each part you will listen to will be announced on the tape. Listen carefully to each listening section and then circle the correct answer for each question in that section.

What's This Story About?

SECTION A

1. Fulghum says,
   a. "How about some good news for a change?"
   b. "How about some bad news for a change?"

2. Fulghum reports that many people say
   a. you can't trust anyone anymore.
   b. you can trust everyone all the time.

3. Fulghum says many people believe that doctors, salesmen, and politicians are all
   a. very honest.
   b. out to rip you off.

4. When Fulghum says, "It ain't necessarily so," he means
   a. you can still trust some people.
   b. everyone really is dishonest.

SECTION B

5. The man who tested the theory was named
   a. Steve Brill.
   b. Steve Chill.

6. He posed as a
   a. poor foreigner.
   b. well-to-do foreigner.

7. Brill got into several dozen taxis in New York City to see
    a. all the big buildings.
    b. how many drivers would cheat him.

8. His friends predicted that
    a. no taxi driver would try to cheat him.
    b. many taxi drivers would try to cheat him.

SECTION C

9. He found out that
    a. only one out of 37 drivers tried to cheat him.
    b. 37 drivers tried to cheat him.

10. Some drivers refused to take him to his destination because
    a. it was so close he could walk there.
    b. they thought he didn't have enough money.

11. Some drivers warned him that
    a. New York was full of crooks so he should be careful.
    b. taxi rides were very expensive.

SECTION D

12. Fulghum says we will continue to hear stories about bad doctors, police, and politicians because
    a. they are the exceptions.
    b. everyone is like that.

13. The Gallup survey showed that
    a. 70 percent of the people believe that most people can be trusted most of the time.
    b. 10 percent of the people believe that most people can be trusted most of the time.

14. When Fulghum says, "Who says people are no damn good? What kind of talk is that?," he believes that
    a. more people are good than bad.
    b. more people are bad than good.

Listen again and check your answers. Share your answers with your partner. Then check your answers with the whole class and discuss any differences of opinion.

Listen Again

In this listening section, you will listen to the complete essay again, but this time there will be no pauses or narration between each section.

The sentences below contain information about the essay you just heard. In every sentence, there is some information that is not true about the essay. The information that is not true is <u>underlined</u>. The sentences are listed in the order that the information is heard on the tape. As you listen to the essay again, cross out the incorrect information and write the correct information above it.

Here are the sentences for you to change. Get ready to focus on the correct answer as you listen to the tape again.

1. Fulghum wants to tell you some <u>bad</u> news for a change.

2. Fulghum says that we often hear the phrase "you <u>can</u> trust anyone."

3. Fulghum says people think that doctors, merchants, and salespeople are all out to <u>help</u> you.

4. A man named Steve Brill tested this idea with <u>bus</u> drivers.

5. Brill pretended he didn't speak <u>Spanish</u> well.

6. Brill said that only <u>five</u> drivers cheated him.

7. Fulghum says that many bad people are on the news, but these people are the <u>usual</u>.

8. A recent <u>message</u> by Gallup shows that 70 percent of people believe that most people can be trusted most of the time.

Listen to the tape again and check your answers with the rest of the class.

Class Activities

What Do You Think?

Discuss with your class the answers to the following questions.

1. Why do you think Fulghum used this story as an example of good news?

2. What do you think about Steve Brill's experiment with the taxi drivers? Do you think it was an interesting experiment? Why or why not?

3. Why do you think Steve Brill's friends predicted that all the taxi drivers would try to cheat him?

4. Were you surprised that only one taxi driver tried to cheat him? Why or why not?

5. Do you agree or disagree with people who think that most people can be trusted most of the time? Explain why you feel this way.

Personal Creations: Opinion Polls

In this essay, Fulghum introduces the idea of opinion polls—a group of questions that people answer about their opinions on different things. Opinion polls are very popular in the United States. American companies take polls to find out what customers want to buy. Politicians take polls to find out what subjects are most important to voters. TV and radio stations take polls to find out what kinds of programs people want to listen to or watch.

In this activity, you will create your own opinion poll. Think about some of the things you don't understand about America or about the country you are living in now. Write down two or three questions to ask people about these things. You can ask questions about the way the government works or why there is so much crime or drugs. Here are a few examples.

1. In your opinion, why do you think Americans have so many guns?

2. What is your opinion about violence on TV?

3. What is your opinion of our president's economic plan?

Write your three questions on a piece of paper. Take your paper to three Americans or three people living in your present country, and ask them these three questions in each of your interviews. Take notes on the interview. After all the students have completed their interviews, give an oral or written report to the class.

Reflections: About Reporting the News—Good or Bad

The way newspapers, TV, and radio report the news is different from country to country. In the United States, freedom to express popular or unpopular opinions is protected by the U.S. Constitution. The right for every citizen to have freedom of speech is the first statement in the Bill of Rights, which is part of the U.S. Constitution.

Some immigrants in the United States are surprised by the wide variety of subjects and opinions they read about in the paper or see on TV. They are not used to watching shows or reading about personal subjects such as family health or political problems.

In addition, some immigrants have expressed the opinion that they think American news organizations have too much freedom: they should not report all the personal information about politicians or movie stars—and sometimes even about the government itself. These people say that too much freedom of information will make the government weak and perhaps weaken the people as well.

How do you feel about the freedom of the newspapers, TV, and radio in the United States or in the country where you are now living? Do you think it is very free or not free enough? Do you think there is a problem with too much freedom?

In your country, was there a lot of freedom to report the news? Describe the subjects written about in the newspapers and on some of the TV and radio programs in your country. Was the news reporting similar to or very different from the United States—or from the country where you now live? Do you think the news reporting was very open or closed? Explain your answer.

Dictation

Listen and fill in the missing words.

A man named _____ Brill tested the _____ .

In New York, with _____ drivers. Brill _____ as

a _____-____-_____ foreigner with little knowledge of _____ .

And he got into several dozen taxis around ____ _____ _____

to see how many drivers would _____ him. His friends

_____ in advance that most would _____ advantage of

him in some _____ .

Speaking of Culture: In Your Own Words

As we saw from José's and Mark's conversation in **Speaking of Culture** in Chapter 1, it is often difficult for some immigrants to get used to asking questions and giving their opinions in class. It can also be surprising to many newcomers that U.S. teachers are also very strict about having students write about their own ideas—not about the ideas of the teacher or the textbook. In addition, teachers expect students to use their <u>own</u> words when they answer questions and not to copy answers word for word from a book.

In this lesson, you will meet José again. This time he is having a conversation with his history teacher, Mrs. Segal. They are talking about a homework paper José wrote last week. Here's the conversation.

José:	Mrs. Segal, did you have a chance to check my paper about U.S. economics yet?
Mrs. Segal:	Yes I did, José.
José:	Well, how was the paper?
Mrs. Segal:	Well, your answers were very good, but I noticed that the words you used were exactly the ones in our textbook.
José:	That's right! So, I guess that means I have all the correct answers?
Mrs. Segal:	Well, yes and no.
José:	I don't understand.
Mrs. Segal:	Let me try to explain. As you know, the subject of this class is history, and our goal is for you to learn all about this subject. But teachers here do not expect that when they give students questions to answer, there is only one "correct" answer. We like to have students learn all the information and material about a particular subject and then be able to answer questions with their own opinion, not only with the opinion in the book.
José:	You mean you want me to read all the material and then write what I think about it?
Mrs. Segal:	Yes, that's what I mean.

José:	Well, I did that. I agree with what the book says.
Mrs. Segal:	There's an additional problem to solve, José. We do not expect students to copy the exact words from any book. We call that "plagiarism," a word that means taking another person's words and saying that they are your words. Plagiarism is against the law here.
José:	So, let me see if I understand. First I read all the information about a subject. Then I think about how I feel about the subject. Then I write about it using my own words, not the exact words in the book.
Mrs. Segal:	That's right, José. And please also remember that if a teacher asks for your opinion and your opinion is different from the teacher's or the textbook's, you can still write about your own ideas. Your ideas do not have to be the same as the teacher's or the book's.
José:	This is so different from my country. It's very hard to get used to it. What should I do about my paper?
Mrs. Segal:	I'll give you back your paper and you can do it over again. This time, please answer the questions with your own ideas and in your own words.
José:	Thank you for the opportunity to do it again. I really need a lot of practice with this new kind of approach.

Now answer these questions.

1. Do you think Mrs. Segal was right to let José do the homework over again? Why or why not?

2. Have you or someone you know ever had an experience similar to José's? If yes, describe the situation.

3. In your country, would the teachers expect you to write papers the way Mrs. Segal described or the way that José expected?

When the circus comes to town, be there.
—Robert Fulghum
<u>It Was on Fire When I Lay Down on It</u>

$\mathcal{L}$ook at the chapter title, the picture, and the quotation below the picture. What do you think this chapter is about? What does the picture tell you about the subject?

*C*hapter Preview

About Advice

Although many people will tell you that you can't get anything for free, that's not always true about advice. Advice is something many people like to give even if you haven't asked for it. Friends and neighbors are very happy to give you advice about a good movie to see, the newest fashion to wear, the best food to eat, or how much and what kind of exercise is best, even if you haven't asked for their advice.

We can make jokes about the free advice people give us, but sometimes we really need to go to experts for advice. If we have a serious health or family problem, we usually have to go to a lawyer, a doctor, or another health professional who charges a fee for advice and service. But whether we listen to free advice from friends and neighbors or pay a professional expert, advice is usually something we can get easily in most places.

Interviewing Your Partner

Sit in groups of four students. Name each member of the group in the following way: Student A, Student B, Student C, and Student D. Students A and B should interview each other. Students C and D should interview each other.

Ask your partner the following interview questions and take notes on the answers.

1. Think about the conversations you had with people over the last few days. Did you receive or give any advice to any of these people? Describe this conversation to your partner.

   _____

   _____

2. Think about the last time you went to a doctor. What advice did the doctor give you?

   _____

   _____

3. Which do you like most—to give advice to other people or to get advice from other people? Describe a situation that shows this.

_____

_____

4. Think about the people who have advised you about important decisions you had to make. In your opinion, what was the best advice anyone ever gave you? What was the worst advice? Share these stories with your partner.

_____

_____

5. Many cultures use proverbs to give advice and to teach a lesson. Read over the following proverbs with your partner. Discuss what you think the meanings of the proverbs are. Then talk about if you agree or disagree with the advice.

PROVERBS:

a. Two heads are better than one.

b. A bird in the hand is worth two in the bush.

c. Never wait until tomorrow if you can do something today.

Do you have proverbs in your country that have similar meanings? Describe them to your partner. Do you remember other proverbs from your culture that give advice? If so, what are they?

Reporting Your Information to the Group

Read over the notes you took about your partner. Then tell the group all about your partner's answers.

Telling or Writing the Group Report

(Optional)

Follow the instructions for this exercise in Chapter 1 (pages 5–6).

$\mathcal{V}$ocabulary Preview

Words and Phrases

Before listening to the essay, let's preview some specific vocabulary words you will hear. In this section, each new vocabulary word is listed with its definition beside it, followed by a sample sentence containing the new word or words. If the sample sentence is taken directly from the essay you will hear, the sentence is marked with quotation marks.

WORDS or PHRASES	MEANING
1. the Ten Commandments	according to the Bible, ten laws that God gave Moses for all the people to follow (Example: **The Ten Commandments** are the main rules in the Bible.)
2. Moses	a famous leader of the Israelites in the Bible (Example: **Moses** brought the people the Ten Commandments.)
3. to take the consequences	to live with the results of one's action (Example: "Do it or **take the consequences**.")
4. the ultimate	the best or the most extreme (Example: The people felt that the new museum was **the ultimate** in design.)
5. good-humored	describing someone who is in a good mood or looks at something in a light way (Example: Joe was **good-humored** about the car accident even though the repair bills were high.)

WORDS or PHRASES	MEANING
6. a cynic	a pessimist; a person who is not hopeful and expects bad results from people and things (Example: His friends called John **a cynic** because he never expected anything good to happen.)
7. middle ground	describing a philosophy that is in between two opposing sides (Example: "As a **middle ground**, I offer Fulghum's Recommendations.")
8. ironclad	describing something that can't be changed easily (Example: The principal created **ironclad** rules that all students had to obey.)
9. despairing	extremely sad, not hopeful (Example: After her husband's death, all her thoughts were **despairing**.)
10. reunion	an activity or an event that brings people together after a long time (Example: I met my high school friends for the first time in ten years at a class **reunion** yesterday.)
11. scenic route	the road to travel on with the best views to look at (Example: "Always take the **scenic route**.")
12. a beggar	a person on the street who begs for money or food (Example: "Give at least something to any **beggar** who asks.")

Vocabulary Quick-Check Review

Check your understanding of the new words and phrases introduced in this chapter by matching the words in column A with their closest definition in Column B.

Column A	Column B
1. ____ Moses	a. not hopeful
2. ____ the Ten Commandments	b. the road with beautiful views
3. ____ take the consequences	c. a pessimist
4. ____ a beggar	d. describing someone in a good mood
5. ____ the ultimate	e. an event where people who haven't seen each other in a long time meet
6. ____ good-humored	f. an important man in the Bible
7. ____ middle ground	g. describing something that is hard to change
8. ____ ironclad	h. the best
9. ____ despairing	i. accept the results of your action
10. ____ reunion	j. a person who asks for food or money
11. ____ scenic route	k. a philosophy between two opposing ideas
12. ____ a cynic	l. laws in the Bible

*E*ssay Preview

In this essay, Fulghum talks about general rules that people should follow to have a good life. On the one hand, he mentions the Ten Commandments. According to the Bible, God gave these rules to inform people how to live a proper life. Although these ten rules are strict, they show that God has confidence that people will follow the rules and do the right things in their lives.

On the other hand, Fulghum mentions Murphy's Law, a humorous rule that does not show confidence in people. Murphy's Law says that if there is a chance for something wrong to happen, then the wrong thing (<u>not</u> the <u>right</u> thing) will definitely happen.

Fulghum decides he should write his own rules of life, which he calls "Fulghum's Recommendations." He thinks that if you follow his recommendations, you will do the right thing and live a good life. Can you guess any recommendations on his list? (Go back to the picture and quotation on the first page of this chapter for one idea that is on his list.)

$\mathcal{F}$ocused Listening

Look over the following questions before you listen to the tape. This will give you an idea of what information to focus on while listening to the essay the first time. The title and the section of each part you will listen to will be announced on the tape. Listen carefully to each listening section, and then circle the correct answer for each question in that section.

What's This Story About?

SECTION A

1. Fulghum says he will talk about something
   a. between the Ten Commandments and Murphy's Law.
   b. between the Ten Commandments and the Bible.

2. Fulghum says that God gave Moses the Ten Commandments
   a. on a tall mountain in the desert.
   b. at the beach.

3. Fulghum says that God was serious about these laws and that if the people did not follow the laws,
   a. nothing would happen.
   b. they would take the consequences.

SECTION B

4. Murphy was the ultimate
   a. good-humored cynic.
   b. optimist.

5. Murphy's Law says that no matter what you do,
   a. things always come out right.
   b. things always come out wrong.

SECTION C

6. Fulghum's Recommendations are
   a. not about God or Murphy.
   b. about God and Murphy.

7. How many recommendations are on Fulghum's list right now?
   a. Nine.
   b. Eleven.

8. Fulghum recommends
   a. never buying lemonade.
   b. always buying lemonade.

9. Fulghum also recommends
   a. voting when you can.
   b. never voting when you can.

10. He thinks that anytime you can vote,
    a. don't do it.
    b. do it.

11. He thinks time is
    a. not important.
    b. more important than money.

12. He recommends that when you travel, take the
    a. shortest route.
    b. scenic route.

13. When you see a beggar, Fulghum recommends that you should
    a. look the other way.
    b. always give him or her money.

14. Always be somebody's
    a. Valentine.
    b. friend.

15. When the circus comes to town, Fulghum says:
    a. "Be there."
    b. "Stay home."

Listen again and check your answers. Share your answers with your partner. Then check your answers with the whole class and discuss any differences of opinion.

Listen Again

In this listening section, you will listen to the complete essay again, but this time there will be no pauses or narration between each section.

The sentences below contain information about the essay you just heard. In every sentence, there is some information that is not true about the essay. The information that is not true is <u>underlined</u>. The sentences are listed in the order that the information is heard on the tape. As you listen to the essay again, cross out the incorrect information and write the correct information above it.

Here are the sentences for you to change. Get ready to focus on the correct answer as you listen to the tape again.

1. Fulghum says that his advice fits somewhere between the <u>Eight</u> Commandments and Murphy's Law.

2. Fulghum says that God <u>ordered</u> Moses to the top of the mountain.

3. Fulghum says that God handed Moses some memos with <u>weak</u> words on them.

4. Fulghum thinks the meaning of the Commandments was "Do it or take the <u>money</u>."

5. Murphy's Law is a rule that says that if anything <u>right</u> can happen, it will happen.

6. Fulghum offers a list he calls "Fulghum's <u>warnings</u>."

7. Fulghum advises people to buy <u>a radio</u> from any kid selling it.

8. Fulghum also advises that we should all be someone's <u>brother</u>.

Listen to the tape again and check your answers with the rest of the class.

*C*lass Activities

What Do You Think?

Discuss with your class the answers to the following questions.

1. In general, what do you think about Fulghum's Recommendations? Which of the recommendations do you think are good advice? Are there any recommendations that you think are not good advice? Tell your partner the answers to these questions.

2. Three of Fulghum's Recommendations are about activities that happen on the street—buying lemonade from any child who is selling it, giving money to street musicians, and giving money to anyone who asks for it. Is streetlife common in your country? If yes, describe typical streetlife activities to your partner.

3. Fulghum adds, "Anytime you can vote on anything, vote." Why do you think Fulghum included this recommendation on his list?

4. Do you agree or disagree with Fulghum's recommendation to give money to "any beggar who asks"? Tell your partner how you feel about this.

5. Fulghum talks about going to the circus when it comes to your town. Was there a circus or were there other types of shows that used to come to your town once or a few times a year? Describe these activities to your partner.

Personal Creations: Your Own Recommendations

Fulghum's list of recommendations includes such things as buying lemonade, going to high school reunions, and being someone's valentine—all important parts of American popular culture.

Think about things in your former country or your present country that you think are important for people who live there, such as celebrating special holidays or customs. Then create a list of three of your own recommendations.

My Own Recommendations:

1. _____

2. _____

3. _____

Reflections: Time or Money?

Fulghum thinks that many people in the United States spend so much time earning money that they don't spend enough time being with their families, relaxing, or helping other people.

In your country, which do people think is more important: time or money? Why do you think this is true?

Which do you think is more important for you: a chance to make more money or a chance to have more time to spend any way you like? Share your ideas with your partner.

Dictation

Listen and fill in the missing words.

What I am about to _____ fits in someplace between
the _____ Commandments and Murphy's _____ .

_____ , you will recall, invited old _____
up on a tall mountain in the _____ and
handed him a _____ of solid-gold memos
with some powerful words on them. _____ .
God didn't say, "Hey, here are ten pretty good _____ ,
see what you think." No. Commandments. _____ it or
_____ the consequences.

In his list of recommendations, Fulghum includes "attend the twenty-fifth reunion of your high school class." High school reunions are an important part of American life. Students who graduated from high school together often get together after ten years, twenty-five years, or even fifty years to have a celebration and bring back memories of their high school days.

High school years are a very important part of American teenagers' process of growing up. When boys and girls celebrate their thirteenth birthday, they become teenagers and begin to plan their future career choices and if and where they will go to college. Unlike many other countries where students go to school, get married, and live in the same town or city where they grew up, American teenagers know that they will have to think about moving away from home and going to a different city or state for school or jobs. For this reason, friendships during the high school years are very strong because the students give support to one another. One reason the high school reunions are important is because it brings people together who haven't seen each other in many years.

Here's a conversation between Rosa, an immigrant from Mexico, and Diane, a co-worker in the same accounting office in Boston. It's Friday afternoon, and Diane and Rosa are talking about their plans for the weekend.

Diane: Rosa, do you have any plans for the weekend?

Rosa: Yes. My sister and her husband and kids are coming to my house on Sunday. We'll have a big dinner, and her kids and mine can have a chance to play together. How about you?

Diane: Well, Saturday night is my twenty-fifth high school reunion. It's going to be in New York City. My husband and I will drive six hours on Saturday to be there.

Roas: Why do you want to take such a long trip?

Diane: It's really important to me. I haven't seen some of my high school friends for many years. It's very exciting to have a chance to see everyone again. Some of the people coming to the reunion are flying from other states such as California, Texas, and Washington. It means a lot to everyone.

Rosa: Why is it in New York?

Diane: I was born in New York and lived there until I went to college in Boston. During college, I met my husband, Jack. We both finished college here, got married, and got jobs here.

Rosa: Weren't your parents upset that you moved away from home?

Diane: At the beginning they were upset. But they knew the program I wanted to study was here in Boston, not in New York. They had to try to get used to it.

Rosa: Aren't you nervous to see people you haven't seen for twenty-five years?

Diane: A little, but it's important for other reasons, too. The twenty-five-year reunion marks a special time in your life, like getting married and having your first job. The reunion is a chance for us to look back to see where we came from and where we are now with our hopes, dreams, and even our personalities. We naturally begin thinking about the direction our lives have taken, and how some things change but other things stay the same.

Rosa: It really sounds like a wonderful opportunity for you, Diane. I hope you have a good time. I look forward to hearing all about it on Monday.

Diane: I'll be happy to tell you all about it.

Now answer these questions.

1. Why was the twenty-fifth high school reunion so important to Diane? Have you ever had a similar experience? Tell your partner about it.

2. In your country is it common to go to school, work, and live in the same town or city for most of your life? Describe this situation to your partner.

3. Do you still see or talk with your closest high school friends? Are these friendships still important to you now? Why?

Chapter 7

EVERYDAY MIRACLES

My grandfather . . . blesses . . . each day when he takes himself off to bed, having eaten and not been eaten once again.

—*Robert Fulghum*
All I Need To Know I Learned In Kindergarten

$\mathcal{L}$ook at the chapter title, the picture, and the quotation below the picture. What do you think this chapter is about? What does the picture tell you about the subject? Go back to Chapter 1 for more ideas about "wonder."

*C*hapter Preview

About Wonder and Miracles

The word "wonderful" means full of wonder. We are "full of wonder" when we see or hear something that amazes us. We are full of wonder when we hear the first cry of a newborn baby or watch the baby's first steps on the way to becoming an adult. When we feel happy, we feel "wonder-full."

The events that fill us with wonder are now popularly called "miracles." These everyday events of mystery and beauty are all around us. For example, think about the miracle that happens when our boss raises our salary or when the apples on an apple tree keep growing several months after the apple season has passed. Or even the process of dreaming at night, which is still a mystery to scientists. It has often been found that when a person becomes aware of and appreciates all these small miracles in life, then that person will discover more and more miracles in his or her life.

Interviewing Your Partner

Sit in groups of four students. Name each member of the group in the following way: Student A, Student B, Student C, and Student D. Students A and B should interview each other. Students C and D should interview each other.

Ask your partner the following interview questions and take notes on the answers.

1. Have you recently seen or heard about an event that filled you with wonder? Describe that event to your partner.

   _____

   _____

2. Do you agree or disagree that our everyday lives are filled with miracles? Describe to your partner why you feel this way.

   _____

   _____

3. The author Lewis Carroll is famous for two books about a girl named Alice who has many strange adventures. In *Alice in Wonderland*, Alice becomes the size of a giant and shrinks to the size of a mouse. She also goes to many odd places and meets many animals and fantastic creatures. Think about the meaning of the word "wonder" and then try to decide why the title of the book is *Alice in Wonderland*. Describe to your partner why you think the book has this title.

_____

_____

4. A saying states: "If you want to see a miracle, you must be patient." What do you think this means? Tell your partner what you think.

_____

_____

5. In another essay, Fulghum tells his readers: "I and You—we are . . . rich, large, living, breathing miracles" (*It Was on Fire When I Lay Down on It*, p. 70). Describe to your partner what you think he means.

_____

_____

Reporting Your Information to the Group

Read over the notes you took about your partner. Then tell the group all about your partner's answers.

Telling or Writing the Group Report

(Optional)

Follow the instructions for this exercise in Chapter 1 (pages 5–6).

*V*ocabulary Preview

Words and Phrases

Before listening to the essay, let's preview some specific vocabulary words you will hear. In this section, each new vocabulary word is listed with its definition beside it, followed by a sample sentence containing the new word or words. If the sample sentence is taken directly from the essay you will hear, the sentence is marked with quotation marks.

WORDS or PHRASES	MEANING
1. a fan	a person who greatly admires another person or group, such as a singer or a sports team (Example: I'm **a fan** of the New York Yankees baseball team.)
2. amateurs	people with a special skill who use that skill for pleasure without being paid for it (Example: We enjoy gardening, but we are all **amateurs**.)
3. small scale	something done without a lot of advertising or notice being paid to it (Example: "My grandfather is a fan of amateurs and **small scale**.")
4. Murphy's Law	a pessimistic philosophy saying that if something wrong can happen, it will happen (Example: **Murphy's Law** is not always true.)
5. momentarily suspended	stopped for a short time. (Example: "Every once in a while the fundamental laws of the universe seem to be **momentarily suspended**.")
6. lump	something shaped like a ball (Example: There was a **lump** on the right side of his knee.)

WORDS or PHRASES	MEANING
7. benign	not dangerous (Example: I was happy to hear that the lump the doctors took out in surgery was **benign**.)
8. fell neatly into place	worked the way it was supposed to (Example: After I thought awhile about how to write the poem, all the words **fell neatly into place**.)
9. bliss	great happiness (Example: My wife and I were in **bliss** when our grandson was born.)
10. a miracle	an event that happens with surprising positive results; an event that cannot be explained by things we usually know are true (Example: It was a **miracle** that no one died in the plane crash.)
11. a rubber check	a check that is written when there is not enough money in the bank to pay for it (Example: The shopowner discovered Joe had given her a worthless **rubber check** and had left the country in a hurry.)
12. fundamental	basic (Example: Every once in a while the **fundamental** laws of the universe seem to be momentarily suspended.)

Vocabulary Quick-Check Review

Check your understanding of the new words and phrases introduced in this chapter by matching the words in column A with their closest definition in Column B.

Column A	Column B
1. _____ a fan	a. worked the way it's supposed to
2. _____ amateurs	b. shaped like a ball
3. _____ small scale	c. things always go wrong
4. _____ lump	d. stopped for a short time
5. _____ benign	e. great happiness
6. _____ Murphy's Law	f. someone who greatly admires someone else
7. _____ momentarily suspended	g. not dangerous
8. _____ bliss	h. something done without a lot of advertising
9. _____ fell neatly into place	i. people who like to perform a special skill and don't get paid to do it
10. _____ fundamental	j. without value
11. _____ a miracle	k. basic
12. _____ a rubber check	l. unexplained or surprising event

*E*ssay Preview

In this essay, Fulghum's grandfather asks Fulghum to take him to a high school football game. His grandfather enjoys watching amateur sports games, not big professional ones. Fulghum and his grandfather think this is a small miracle, and they enjoy being there to share it.

Fulghum talks about other small miracles in our lives, such as getting good news at the doctor's office when you were afraid of bad news and glasses that drop in the sink and don't break. What other small miracles do you think Fulghum might talk about in this essay?

$\mathcal{F}$ocused Listening

Look over the following questions before you listen to the tape. This will give you an idea of what information to focus on while listening to the essay the first time. The title and the section of each part you will listen to will be announced on the tape. Listen carefully to each listening section, and then circle the correct answer for each question in that section.

What's This Story About?

SECTION A

1. Grandfather Sam asked Fulghum to take him to
   a. a soccer game.
   b. a football game.

2. Grandfather Sam is a fan of
   a. professional football stars.
   b. amateurs and small scale.

3. Grandfather Sam is interested in times
   a. when miracles happen to ordinary people.
   b. when good things happen to bad people.

4. Grandfather Sam likes things
   a. small scale.
   b. large scale.

SECTION B

5. Grandfather Sam says
   a. Murphy's Law doesn't always hold.
   b. Murphy's Law is always true.

6. Sometimes the laws of the universe are momentarily suspended and
   a. everything goes right.
   b. everything goes wrong.

SECTION C

7. Fulghum talks about dropping a glass in the sink
   a. and not breaking it.
   b. and breaking it.

8. Fulghum talks about luck preventing a
   a. holiday.
   b. rubber check.

9. Fulghum talks about a lump that is
   a. dangerous.
   b. benign.

SECTION D

10. Fulghum says small miracles occur for people day by day when
    a. some little piece falls neatly into place.
    b. only bad things happen.

11. Fulghum says bliss is a day when
    a. life just works.
    b. life doesn't work.

SECTION E

12. Fulghum's grandfather blesses God each day for
    a. having eaten and not having been eaten.
    b. having an animal to eat.

13. Fulghum's grandfather also blesses God for
    a. what goes wrong.
    b. what goes right.

Listen again and check your answers. Share your answers with your partner. Then check your answers with the whole class and discuss any differences of opinion.

Listen Again

In this listening section, you will listen to the complete essay again, but this time there will be no pauses or narration between each section.

The sentences below contain information about the essay you just heard. In every sentence, there is some information that is not true about the essay. The incorrect information is <u>underlined</u>. The sentences are listed in the order that the information is heard on the tape. As you listen to the essay again, cross out the incorrect information and write the correct information above it.

Here are the sentences for you to change. Get ready to focus on the correct answer as you listen to the tape again.

1. Grandfather Sam called up on <u>Thursday</u>.

2. Grandfather Sam likes <u>large scale</u>.

3. Grandfather Sam is interested in times when miracles happen to <u>rich</u> people.

4. Murphy's <u>Alphabet</u> does not always hold.

5. Ever drop a glass and have it <u>break</u> nine times?

6. Grandfather Sam blessed God for having eaten and not having been <u>late</u>.

7. Grandfather Sam appreciates all the things that go <u>wrong</u>.

Listen to the tape again and check your answers with the rest of the class.

*C*lass Activities

What Do You Think?

Discuss with your class the answers to the following questions.

1. How do you feel about Grandfather Sam? Do you feel he is an optimist or a pessimist? Describe to your partner what you liked and what you didn't like about Grandfather Sam.

2. Why did Grandfather Sam like to see amateur football games and not the big professional games on TV?

3. What was Grandfather Sam's opinion about Murphy's Law?

4. Fulghum describes a few lucky miracles that happen to people every day, such as dropping and not breaking a glass and going to the doctor and hearing good news about a possibly dangerous health problem. Have you ever had one of these experiences or something similar? Describe that event to your partner.

5. What does Grandfather Sam mean when he says he blesses God for "having eaten and not having <u>been</u> eaten"?

Personal Creations: A Family Tree

Many American families keep a record of their "family tree"—a chart that shows all the generations of a family, the names of the people, when and where they were born, their children, and whom everyone married. This chart is usually divided into two parts—the mother's side of the family and the father's side.

Here's an example of how three generations of a Chinese family named Liang might look on a "family tree":

Look at the chart and answer the questions below and on the next page.

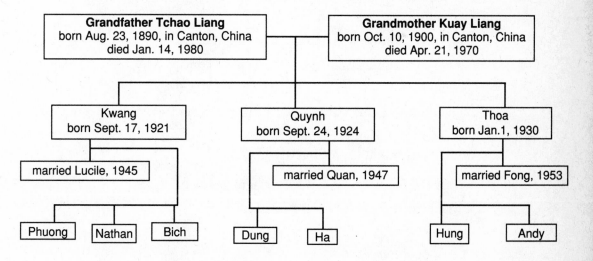

1. What was the name of Thoa's father?

_____

2. Does Thoa have any sisters or brothers? If so, what are their names?

    _____

3. Which child of Tchao and Kuay had the most children?

    _____

    What are the names of these children?

    _____

Think about your family history. Go back three generations on your father's or mother's side and create a form with the names and dates of your family members. When everyone in the class is finished, find out which student has the most relatives and which student has the least relatives.

Dictation

Listen and fill in the missing words.

My grandfather Sam called me up last _____
to ask me if I'd take him to a _____ _____ .
Grandfather likes small-town _____ _____
football. Grandfather is a _____ of amateurs
and _____ _____ . Some people are concerned
about how it is that _____ things happen to _____
people, and there are those who are concerned about
how _____ things happen to _____ people. But my
grandfather is interested in those times when _____
happen to _____ people. Here again, he _____
small scale.

Reflections: About Families

In this essay, Fulghum tells about his grandfather and the lessons Fulghum has learned about life from him. The story shows us the close relationship and understanding between them.

In the United States today, it is uncommon for family members from different generations to live in the same house or even to live near one another. Before the twentieth century, most American families were extended families—different generations of the same family living together. But today, the most common style of family is the nuclear family, in which only the parents and their children live together.

In your country, which type of family—extended or nuclear—is most common? Did you grow up in an extended family or in a nuclear family? Describe to your partner the kind of family in which you grew up.

Which type of family life do you prefer—extended or nuclear? Describe why you feel this way to your partner.

Speaking of Culture

In this essay, Fulghum takes his grandfather to a high school football game. Football is a very popular game in America. It is also a very competitive sport—a sport where one player tries to be better than other players. Some experts who study American society have said that the game of football reflects the competitiveness of life in America. Although football is a team sport and all players must work together for the same goals, each individual player has a large responsibility for taking care of his own job in the game. In the United States, all Americans earning a certain income pay taxes to keep their country united and strong, and in that sense they are on the same team working together for the same goal. But they also must be successful in their individual jobs, where they are often competing with one another.

There is great competition in the United States for jobs, and this competition is often difficult for newcomers to get used to. Here's a conversation between Seng, an immigrant who came from mainland China five years ago, and his co-worker Larry at an electronics assembly plant.

Larry: Hi. Seng. What's up? You look upset.

Seng: I have a problem with my son.

Larry: What happened? Is he hurt?

Seng: No, it's not like that. He graduated a few months ago from college with a degree in electrical engineering.

Larry:	What's the problem?
Seng:	He can't find a job. He told me that there are so many people applying for the same job that there is no room for him. He got good grades in school, so I don't understand how this can be true.
Larry:	Seng, what your son told you about American jobs is true. Getting a job here depends a lot on the economy and on how many job openings there are. If the economy is strong, companies will usually hire more new workers. In a slow economy, companies watch their budgets and cut down on their number of employees.
Seng:	He had good letters from all his professors. In China, these letters would have given him the best job with the highest salary.
Larry:	American companies like to hire workers with good letters of recommendations, but the letters cannot create a job opening if there isn't any.
Seng:	In China when my oldest son graduated college, the government guaranteed him a job.
Larry:	It's just not like that here. The federal government does not make those decisions for individual people. In general, the people who wrote our Constitution wanted to make sure that the government doesn't have the power to control our lives. Americans wanted to have the right to make decisions about their own lives. I guess there's a good side and a bad side to all forms of government.
Seng:	I like China's way about jobs better.
Larry:	Seng, I think it's helpful to realize that Americans who have lived their whole lives here also have to live with the same problem that your son has. The economy is the same for everyone. Learning to live independently in this country is the price we pay for all our freedom.
Seng:	I feel very disappointed about my son and his job, but I will try to get used to it.

Now answer these questions.

1. In your country, what are the most common ways that people get jobs? Describe these ways to your partner.

2. Does the government of your country give jobs automatically to people after they graduate from college? Describe this situation to your partner.

3. In your opinion, which way do you think is better: should individuals be responsible for finding their own jobs, or should they receive help from the government?

Chapter 8

THE MASKS PEOPLE WEAR

The human face communicates.

—*Carol Sivin*
Maskmaking

$\mathcal{L}$ook at the chapter title, the picture, and the quotation below the picture. What do you think this chapter is about? What does the picture tell you about the subject?

*C*hapter Preview

About Masks

Early human records show that masks have been an important part of ceremonies and artwork for thousands of years. Different cultures used masks to express the beliefs of their own society and to change or hide the identity of the person wearing the mask. At times, masks were used to scare bad spirits and prevent bad luck. At other times, masks were used to welcome friendly spirits and invite good luck. Today's very popular American holiday Halloween—a holiday on which children, and sometimes adults, dress in costumes and wear masks—was originally a ceremony to protect individuals from the spirits of the dead.

Masks can hide who we are, and masks can also hide what we are feeling. Have you ever smiled in front of other people when you really felt angry or upset? Can you remember how you felt then? Your smile was a natural mask—a face you put on to hide your feelings underneath. All of us wear these natural masks at different times in our lives. Sometimes our need to hide may seem more important than our need to share.

Interviewing Your Partner

Sit in groups of four students. Name each member of the group in the following way: Student A, Student B, Student C, and Student D. Students A and B should interview each other. Students C and D should interview each other.

Ask your partner the following interview questions and take notes on the answers.

1. Are masks used in any holiday celebrations, traditions, or religious ceremonies in your culture? If yes, tell about these customs. Are masks popular in your culture's theater or other arts? If so, how are they used? Have you ever worn a mask? Describe this situation to your partner.

   _____

   _____

2. In general, which is easiest for you—to share your feelings with other people or to keep your feelings private? Is there any friend or relative you talk to when you are upset? Describe this person to your partner.

_____

_____

3. Are there any emotions you are expected to keep hidden in your culture? If so, what are they?

_____

_____

4. A popular American song from the 1940s is called "Smile." It advises people to "smile though your heart is breaking." Do you think this is good advice? Why or why not? Are there any songs, proverbs, or idioms from your culture about hiding or sharing your feelings? Describe them to your partner.

_____

_____

5. People keep their feelings hidden in many ways. In addition to hiding anger or sadness, people find ways to hide fear. An example is in the popular musical *The King And I*, in which Anna sings that when she is afraid, she whistles so "no one will know I'm afraid." What do you think of Anna's technique? Do you do anything special to help yourself when you feel afraid? If yes, what? Have you ever begun a new experience that made you afraid at the beginning? Share this story with your partner.

_____

_____

Reporting Your Information to the Group

Read over the notes you took about your partner. Then tell the group all about your partner's answers.

Telling or Writing the Group Report

(Optional)

Follow the instructions for this exercise in Chapter 1 (pages 5–6).

$\mathcal{V}$ocabulary Preview

Words and Phrases

Before listening to the essay, let's preview some specific vocabulary words you will hear. In this section, each new vocabulary word is listed with its definition beside it, followed by a sample sentence containing the new word or words. If a sample sentence is taken directly from the essay you will hear, the sentence is marked with quotation marks.

WORDS or PHRASES	MEANING
1. Hide-and-Seek	a popular child's game in which all the children hide and another child tries to find them (Example: "In the early dry dark of an October's Saturday evening, the neighborhood children are playing **Hide-and-Seek**.")
2. to "leave someone to rot"	to leave someone alone by himself or herself (Example: "After a while, we would give up on him, **leaving him to rot** wherever he was.")
3. to show up	to arrive somewhere (Example: "Sooner or later, he would **show up**.")
4. terminal cancer	a particular disease that has no cure (Example: "A man I know found out last year he had **terminal cancer**.")

WORDS or PHRASES	MEANING
5. to suffer	to have any kind of physical or emotional pain (Example: ". . . he didn't want to make his family **suffer**.")
6. sardines	a type of small edible fish, usually packed tightly in a can (also used in this essay as the name of a child's game) (Examples: We ate **sardines** for lunch. The kids like to play the game Sardines.)
7. "It"	in the game Hide-and-Seek, the player who tries to find where the other children are hiding (Example: In "Hide-and-Seek," the person who is "**It**" tries to find all the other children who are hiding.)
8. puppies in a pile	baby dogs on top of one another (Example: The mother dog moved all the **puppies in a pile** next to a tree.)
9. to giggle	to laugh softly (Example: "And pretty soon somebody **giggles** and somebody laughs and everybody gets found.")
10. "olly-olly-oxen-free"	words spoken in the game Hide-and-Seek by any player who gets to a "safe" place before "It" can find him or her (Example: "**Olly-olly-oxen-free**. The kids out in the street are hollering the cry that says, Come on in wherever you are. It's a new game.")

Vocabulary Quick-Check Review

Check your understanding of the new words and phrases introduced in this chapter by matching the words in column A with their closest definition in Column B.

Column A		Column B
1. ____ sardines	a.	to arrive somewhere
2. ____ Hide-and-Seek	b.	to laugh softly
3. ____ puppies in a pile	c.	to leave someone alone
4. ____ to show up	d.	a disease that can't be cured
5. ____ to suffer	e.	small fish often packed tightly in a can
6. ____ to "leave someone to rot"	f.	words used in the children's game Hide-and-Seek when the player gets to a "safe" place before the player who is "It" can find him
7. ____ to giggle	g.	baby dogs on top of each other
8. ____ "olly-olly-oxen-free"	h.	the player who looks for the other players who are hiding in the game Hide-and-Seek
9. ____ "It"	i.	the name of a children's game where one person tries to find the others, who are hiding
10. ____ terminal cancer	j.	to have any kind of pain

*E*ssay Preview

Have you ever heard of Hide-and-Seek? It's a children's game about hiding and finding. Here are a few basic rules of the game.

1. The players choose one person to be "It."
2. The players also choose a location called "safe."
3. "It" closes his or her eyes, and all the other players hide somewhere.
4. After a short time, "It" tries to find all the players.

5. While "It" tries to find the players, each individual player tries to run to the "safe" place before "It" catches (tags) him or her.

6. When the player gets to the "safe" place, he or she yells "Olly-olly-oxen-free."

Fulghum remembers having played this game when he hears children playing Hide-and-Seek outside his house. One day while watching the game, he thinks about a doctor he knew who recently died from terminal cancer. The doctor hid the truth about his illness from his family, and they didn't know he had cancer until he died. When the doctor died and his family learned the truth, they were upset he had never told them. Fulghum thinks the man was hiding so no one could find him, like in the game Hide-and-Seek. Do you think adults play games to hide, just like children? If yes, in what ways?

$\mathcal{F}$ocused Listening

Look over the following questions before you listen to the tape. This will give you an idea of what information to focus on while listening to the essay the first time. The title and the section of each part you will listen to will be announced on the tape. Listen carefully to each listening section, and then circle the correct answer for each question in that section.

What's This Story About?

SECTION A

1. The neighborhood kids are outside playing
   a. in October.
   b. in December.

2. Fulghum says he hasn't played the game Hide-and-Seek for at least
   a. 40 years.
   b. 30 years.

SECTION B

3. Fulghum asks if we ever played the game with a kid who
   a. hid too well.
   b. wore pants and a tie.

4. Fulghum said that if he and his friends couldn't find the player who hid,
    a. they'd give up and leave him alone.
    b. they'd go to the kid's house and wait.

5. Fulghum thinks this kid
    a. hated the game.
    b. might still be hiding.

SECTION C

6. The man who Fulghum learned had had terminal cancer was
    a. a police officer.
    b. a doctor.

7. The person who had the cancer didn't tell his family about it because
    a. he said he didn't want them to suffer.
    b. he kept forgetting to tell them.

8. The family was upset he hadn't told them because
    a. they thought he didn't need them and they didn't have a chance to say good-bye.
    b. they wanted to move far away.

9. Fulghum thinks the person who had the cancer
    a. did the right thing.
    b. hid too well.

10. Fulghum thinks the doctor played Hide and Seek
    a. children's style.
    b. grown-up style.

SECTION D

11. Fulghum likes the game Sardines better than Hide-and-Seek because
    a. the players are altogether in one place and no one is hiding.
    b. he likes to eat sardines.

12. Fulghum advises people whom he thinks have hid too well
    a. to learn how to cooperate and share in the game Sardines.
    b. to go back and hide again.

Listen again and check your answers. Share your answers with your partner. Then check your answers with the whole class and discuss any differences of opinion.

Listen Again

In this listening section, you will listen to the complete essay again, but this time there will be no pauses or narration between each section.

The sentences below contain information about the essay you just heard. In every sentence, there is some information that is not true about the essay. The incorrect information is <u>underlined</u>. The sentences are listed in the order that the information is heard on the tape. As you listen to the essay again, cross out the incorrect information and write the correct information above it.

Here are the sentences for you to change. Get ready to focus on the correct answer as you listen to the tape again.

1. Fulghum is watching the neighborhood children on a <u>Monday</u> evening.

2. Fulghum says that <u>children</u> don't play Hide-and-Seek.

3. Fulghum says that there was always a kid in his neighborhood who <u>spoke</u> too good.

4. A man Fulghum knew found out he had <u>glasses</u>.

5. His family didn't know about his health because he didn't <u>visit</u> them.

6. The family felt <u>good</u> that he didn't say good-bye.

7. The game Fulghum likes better than Hide-and-Seek is called <u>Tuna</u>.

8. Fulghum's advice to people who have hid too well is: "Get <u>lost</u>, kid!"

Listen to the tape again, then check your answers with the rest of the class.

Class Activities

What Do You Think?

Discuss with your class the answers to the following questions.

1. Do you think the doctor was right to keep the information about his illness a secret from his family? Describe why you feel this way.

2. How did the doctor's family feel when they found out he had had cancer and hadn't told them? Has anything like this ever happened to you or someone you know? Describe the situation.

3. Which game do you like better—Hide-and-Seek or Sardines? Describe why you feel this way.

4. Are there any games for children in your culture that are similar to Hide-and-Seek? Tell the class how to play this game.

5. In the United States, many games are popular among adults. Many men and women in the United States play indoor and outdoor sports, like tennis, volleyball, baseball, and basketball. Card games and chess are also very popular. Are there any popular adult games in your country? Describe these games to the class.

Personal Creations: Masks and Costumes from Your Country

An ESL class brings a lot of people together from different cultures and countries. Here's an activity in which you can share your cultural background with other students.

Think about special costumes, masks, or decorations that are used in your culture for celebrations. If you have any examples of these things, bring them to class and tell your classmates when, how, and why they are used. If you don't have the examples to bring to class, create a mask, costume, or decoration that is important in your culture, or find a picture of it in a book or magazine and bring the picture to class. Then talk about the custom or celebration that is connected to it.

Reflections: Hiding or Telling Bad News to a Patient

There are several philosophies about people being told bad news about their health. In general in the United States, most doctors believe that giving the patient as much information as possible—even when it is a serious condition—produces the best results. The doctors believe that it gives the patient the ability to make choices about what therapies to choose. They also believe that the patient will do well if he is able to participate in the process and treatment.

On the other hand, in many other cultures the doctors believe that the best results will come from the patient not knowing the truth about his or her serious condition. The doctors believe that if the patient knows that he or she has a terrible disease, the fear of the disease will prevent the patient from getting better. Sometimes the news is shared only with the patient's family, and sometimes only the doctor knows.

In your culture, which technique is more common—to tell the patient bad news or to keep it a secret? Why do you think it is more common?

If you were a doctor and you found out your patient had a very serious illness, would you tell him/her or would you keep it a secret? Why? Which choice do you think would be the best for the patient? If you had a serious illness, would you want the doctor to tell you the truth or keep it a secret? Describe why you feel this way.

Dictation

Listen and fill in the missing words.

A man I know found out last year he had terminal _____ .

He was a _____ . And he knew about dying, and he didn't

want to make his _____ and friends _____ through that

with him. So he kept his _____ . And he died. And everybody

said how _____ he was to bear his suffering in _____ and not

tell _____ , and so on and so forth. But privately his

_____ and friends said how _____ they were that he didn't

need them, he didn't _____ their strength. And it _____ that

he didn't say _____ .

In this chapter's essay, the family of the doctor who had cancer was hurt and upset that he had kept his illness hidden from the family. They believed that it would have been better for him and the rest of the family to be open about the truth than to hide it.

Many Americans believe that being open about your feelings is better than hiding them. This idea is seen in other areas of current American life, including the workplace. Many newcomers are surprised and confused by the amount of time Americans spend talking about and giving attention to their personal feelings. Here's an example.

Rita is a medical records keeper in a local hospital. This is her first job in America since she left Guatemala. One of her job requirements is to attend Staff Development Programs. Today she received an announcement about Staff Development Programs for the next three months. She has the following conversation with Beth, her co-worker.

Rita: Beth, can I ask you some questions about this announcement?

Beth: Sure. What is it?

Rita: I'm trying to understand something about the programs announced for Staff Development, but some of the titles are really confusing.

Beth: Which ones?

Rita: Here's one I really don't understand. [Rita reads the title out loud.] "Self-Empowerment: Find Out Who You Are and All You Can Be." What is self-empowerment, and why do employees need this?

Beth: Self-empowerment is knowing that you have many wonderful abilities inside you. Learning about how to use these abilities can make you a happier and more successful person. If you understand these abilities and learn how to use them, you will feel more confident and be a better worker.

Rita: Do they think there is something wrong with my work?

Beth: Oh, no. That's not the idea. You know, Americans have a strong belief in improving themselves. In any bookshop you can see hundreds of books to help you improve your life—how to cook better, how to play tennis better, how to manage your children in a better way, etc. The main idea is that learning new things will build your confidence and then everything you do will get better, including your job.

Rita: How do they teach you to know yourself better?

Beth: Usually these programs involve a lot of talking about yourself and your feelings. Workshop leaders ask all the individuals a lot of personal questions about their life, how they feel about their life, and even how they feel about the people in their life. Sometimes they talk to partners; sometimes they tell the whole class.

Rita: I've never talked in front of a group about my feelings. If I feel upset about something, I keep it private or I talk to someone in my family.

Beth: The philosophy is that if you hide your feelings, you create problems inside you. These problems can prevent you from feeling good about yourself. The leaders believe that bringing your angry and hurt feelings into the open will help make these bad feelings disappear. When you throw away these feelings and understand yourself better, you will bring good ideas to everything in your life, including your job.

Rita: I thought the idea of Staff Development Programs would be to teach me more about medical records, not how to talk about my feelings.

Beth: I'm sure this sounds strange to you. It's not really so bad. Sometimes we learn ways that help us get along with other employees, too. That's been very helpful for me. You know, I'm going to the workshop tomorrow night. Can you come, too?

Rita: That's a great idea. I'll feel better if we go together.

Now answer these questions.

1. If you were Rita, do you think you would feel comfortable or uncomfortable about going to the Self-Empowerment Program? Explain.

2. Do you think talking about your feelings in public with other employees can be a good way to improve your work on the job? Why or why not?

3. If you were planning a Staff Development Program for workers, what subjects would you include?

Chapter 9

THE CREATIVE PROCESS

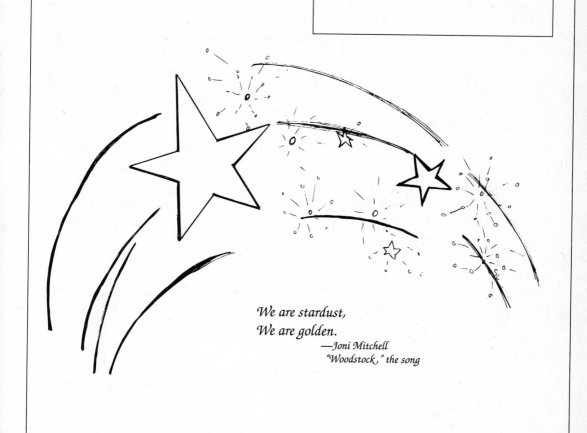

We are stardust,
We are golden.
　　　　—Joni Mitchell
　　　"Woodstock," the song

*L*ook at the chapter title, the picture, and the quotation below the picture. What do you think this chapter is about? What does the picture tell you about the subject?

*C*hapter Preview

About the Creative Process

What is the creative process? It is the step-by-step development of a new idea or object. Examples of the creative process are all around us. Look up at the sky. Watch the clouds as they move and dance into new forms. The clouds' movements are examples of the process, and the new shapes you see and the feelings you experience while watching them are part of the new creation. As another example, think about seeds you've planted in the ground. Planting the seeds began the creative process. The flowers, fruits, or vegetables that grew from the seeds become the creation.

It is not necessary to look at the sky or our gardens to be close to the creative process. Many of the simple things we do every day—such as cooking, reading, and thinking—are parts of creative processes. The growth and development of our children, friends, and family is also part of an active, continuous, creative process. In addition, our bodies are part of a very active creative process. Every minute, our bodies create new chemicals and materials to keep our blood clean and our bodies strong. The next time you develop an idea or begin to make a dream come true, remember at that moment that you, too, are part of a creative process.

Interviewing Your Partner

Sit in groups of four students. Name each member of the group in the following way: Student A, Student B, Student C, and Student D. Students A and B should interview each other. Students C and D should interview each other.

Ask your partner the following interview questions and take notes on the answers.

1. Think about something you have made or created in the last week. It can be something you cooked, something you wrote about, or something you thought about and then did. Think about the steps you followed from the time you began thinking about it to the time you created or did the thing. Tell your partner the thing you created and the steps you followed.

_____

_____

2. In language classes, including ESL, it is common for the teacher to talk to the students about "the writing process." Think about what you do when you write. Write down two steps you follow when you write in your native language and two steps you follow when you write in English. Are the steps the same or different? Describe these steps to your partner. Why do you think writing is called a "process"?

_____

_____

3. In his popular TV show *Cosmos* (meaning the Universe), scientist and writer Carl Sagan tells the listeners many interesting things about nature and the creative process. According to Sagan, most of life on earth is made of the same basic materials. He says that we are made of "starstuff," materials found in all life in the universe. He also says that because all life is so similar, each person is a "mini-universe." What do you think he means when he says we are all a "mini-universe"? Describe your thoughts to your partner.

_____

_____

4. There are many examples of the creative process in our lives. The paragraphs above mention the sky, growing things in the garden, watching your family grow, and building your own hopes and dreams. Think of two more examples of the creative process. Describe these examples to your partner.

_____

_____

5. Many cultures around the world have folktales about the process of the creation of the world. For example, in ancient Egypt there is a folk story that says that the sun god, Ra, started the process of earth's creation. It says, "he separated night from day. The gods came forth from his mouth and man[kind] from his eyes. All things took their birth from him." Does this story remind you of other stories you have heard about the creation of the earth? Do you know any folktales from your culture or another culture that describe the creation of the earth? Share these stories with your partner.

_____

_____

Reporting Your Information to the Group

Read over the notes you took about your partner. Then tell the group all about your partner's answers.

Telling or Writing the Group Report

(Optional)

Follow the directions for this exercise in Chapter 1 (pages 5–6).

*V*ocabulary Preview

Words and Phrases

Before listening to the essay, let's preview some specific vocabulary words you will hear. In this section, each new vocabulary word is listed with its definition beside it, followed by a sample sentence containing the new word or words. If a sample sentence is taken directly from the essay you will hear, the sentence is marked with quotation marks.

WORDS or PHRASES	MEANING
1. resources	all of the available materials people have (Example: "Good friends (I know) finally put their **resources** together and made themselves a child.")
2. godfather	a male selected by the parents to assist in their child's moral education and welfare (Example: Joe and Mayra asked their friend Ted to be their child's **godfather** because they trusted and admired him.)

WORDS or PHRASES	MEANING
3. training wheels	two extra wheels attached to the back wheel of a bicycle to provide balance (Many children in the United States learn to ride a bicycle first with training wheels. The expression also indicates the first steps of a new procedure.)
	(Example: "I introduced him to crayons. Bought the Crayola beginner training set—the short, fat, thick ones with 'training wheels.'")
4. to stare	to look intently at someone with no expression on your face
	(Example: "Mostly he just held it and stared at me.")
5. he got the picture	he understood
	(Example: "I held his hand and made a big red mark with a Crayola on a sheet of newsprint. And WHAM! He got the picture.")
6. a binder	something that holds other things together
	(Example: "Amazing things, Crayolas. Some petroleum-based wax, some dye, a little binder.")
7. oleaginous	describing something that comes from oil or that contains oil
	(Example: "The Binney Company in Pennsylvania makes about two billion of these oleaginous sticks of pleasure every year and exports them to every country in the United Nations.")

WORDS or PHRASES	MEANING
8. a sign of progress	something showing forward movement in thought or action
	(Example: It is **a sign of progress** that our city buses now have equipment to carry customers in wheelchairs.)
9. to indulge yourself	to do the thing you feel like doing
	(Example: When I saw the beautiful box of crayons, I **indulged myself** and bought a box for myself.)
10. to launch	to begin something; to move something high up in space, like a rocket
	(Example: They plan to **launch** the space station in 1999.)
11. sheer bulk	a large amount of things
	(Example: "For **sheer bulk**, there's more art done with Crayolas than with anything else.")
12. absurd	something that doesn't make sense
	(Example: People laughed at Bill's crazy idea for a movie and said it was **absurd**.)

Vocabulary Quick-Check Review

Check your understanding of the new words and phrases introduced in this chapter by matching the words in column A with their closest definition in Column B.

	Column A		**Column B**
1. ____	resources	a.	to do what you want.
2. ____	to stare	b.	he understood.
3. ____	he got the picture	c.	a group of things.
4. ____	a binder	d.	used to help people begin something new
5. ____	oleaginous	e.	something that shows forward movement of a thing or an idea
6. ____	training wheels	f.	to look at
7. ____	to indulge oneself	g.	materials
8. ____	to launch	h.	coming from oil
9. ____	sheer bulk	i.	to send up in the air
10. ____	sign of progress	j.	a large amount
11. ____	absurd	k.	person responsible for education and welfare of a child
12. ____	godfather	l.	doesn't make sense

*E*ssay Preview

In this essay, Fulghum talks about the creative process that occurs when someone draws with Crayola crayons. When Fulghum became a godparent (a person or relative with a very close and special relationship with a family), he gave his new godson a small box of crayons. At first the child didn't know what to do with the crayons, but he soon began drawing with crayons on everything he saw.

Fulghum talks about how surprised he is that such a simple thing as crayons—wax made from petroleum and dyes for color—could bring so much enjoyment to children and adults. He also bought a box of crayons for the parents of his godson, and they like to play with them, too. Fulghum says that every time he gives an adult a box of crayons, the person begins talking about his or her childhood and what he or she did with the crayons as a child.

Fulghum also suggests some unusual ideas for crayons to help bring world peace. What ways can you think of in which crayons could be used for this purpose?

$\mathcal{F}$ocused Listening

Look over the following questions before you listen to the tape. This will give you an idea of what information to focus on while listening to the essay the first time. The title and the section of each part you will listen to will be announced on the tape. Listen carefully to each listening section, and then circle the correct answer for each question in that section.

What's This Story About?

SECTION A

1. Fulghum's good friends put their resources together and
   a. built a house.
   b. had a child.

2. He thinks his job of godfather is
   a. a joke.
   b. serious.

3. Fulghum introduced his godson to
   a. apple pie.
   b. crayons.

4. When Fulghum's godson first tried crayons, he
   a. just stared at Fulghum.
   b. ate them.

5. Finally, after many weeks, Fulghum used a red crayon with his godson, and the godson finally
   a. took a picture.
   b. got the picture.

SECTION B

6. For children, Fulghum thinks that Crayolas plus imagination create
   a. happiness.
   b. good pictures.

7. The Binney Company in Pennsylvania makes
   a. twelve (12) billion crayons a year.
   b. two (2) billion crayons a year.

8. The Binney Company exports Crayolas to
   a. every country in the United Nations.
   b. every country in the world.

9. Since 1937, the green and yellow box of Crayolas
   a. has never changed.
   b. has been changed three (3) times.

10. The only change in Crayola colors is from
    a. "orange" to "sunshine."
    b. "flesh" to "peach."

SECTION C

11. When Fulghum bought a crayon trainer set for his godson, he
    a. bought three (3) sets for his wife.
    b. also bought a set for himself.

12. When he got a set of Crayolas for his godson's parents, he explained
    a. it was for them.
    b. it was for their son.

13. Fulghum says for sheer bulk,
    a. more art is done on walls than on anything else.
    b. more art is done with Crayolas than with anything else.

14. Fulghum thinks that Ronald Reagan, Mikhail Gorbachev, and Fidel Castro
    a. all used crayons.
    b. all used paint.

15. Fulghum thinks that in every country in the world there must be billions of sheets of paper covered with
    a. pictures in crayon.
    b. pictures in ink.

SECTION D

16. Fulghum thinks our next secret weapon should be
    a. an atomic bomb.
    b. a Crayola bomb.

17. When Fulghum's Crayola bomb exploded, it would send millions of
    a. flowers into the air.
    b. parachutes into the air.

18. The things that floated down to earth with the parachutes would be
    a. boxes of Crayolas.
    b. boxes of bombs.

19. Fulghum believes that other people will think his suggestion about the Crayola Bomb is
    a. crazy, silly, and absurd.
    b. a good idea.

20. After Fulghum read a newspaper story about how much the Russians and the U. S. Congress spend for weapons, he knew his idea for a Crayola bomb
    a. is better than using atomic bombs.
    b. is more expensive than using atomic bombs.

Listen again and check your answers. Share your answers with your partner. Then check your answers with the whole class and discuss any differences of opinion.

Listen Again

In this listening section, you will listen to the complete essay again, but this time there will be no pauses or narration between each section.

The sentences below contain information about the essay you just heard. In every sentence, there is some information that is not true about the essay. The incorrect information is <u>underlined</u>. The sentences are listed in the order that the information is heard on the tape. As you listen to the essay again, cross out the incorrect information and write the correct information above it.

Here are the sentences for you to change. Get ready to focus on the correct answer as you listen to the tape again.

1. Fulghum just became the <u>grandfather</u> of his friend's son.

2. Fulghum introduced this child to <u>hamburgers</u>.

3. The <u>McDonald's</u> Company in Pennsylvania makes Crayolas.

4. The company that makes Crayolas changed the color "flesh" to <u>red</u>.

5. Fulghum bought a set of Crayolas for the kid's <u>brothers</u>.

6. Fulghum thinks that Ronald Reagan, Gorbachev, and Fidel Castro all used <u>toothbrushes</u>.

7. Fulghum suggests we use Crayolas to create a Beauty <u>Wall</u>.

Listen to the tape again then check your answers with the rest of the class.

Class Activities

What Do You Think?

Discuss with your class the answers to the following questions.

1. Are Crayola crayons used in your country? How and where are they used? Have you ever used them? Describe your experience with them to your partner.

2. How did you feel about Fulghum giving his godson a box of crayons soon after he was born? Do you think you would do the same thing? Why or why not?

3. Fulghum writes that the only change in Crayola crayons since 1937 is changing the name of the color "flesh" to the color "peach." The color "flesh" means skin color. The color "peach" is a light pink salmon color. The Crayola company changed the name of the color because it realized that there are many skin colors, not only pink or white. Fulghum says that this name change was "a sign of progress." Why do you think Fulghum thought that the company moved forward in some way?

4. How do you feel about Fulghum's idea to create a Crayola bomb? He thinks that using imagination can help us find new ways to solve world problems. Do you agree? Describe your ideas to your partner.

5. Fulghum says that if you give crayons to people, they will use them, but that children and adults use them differently. Mr. Bruce Klowden, owner of a well-known San Diego restaurant called Aesop's Tables, agrees with Fulghum. In this restaurant, on every dining table there are a bundle of crayons and a paper tablecloth. There are no instructions about the crayons, but because they are there people use them. Mr. Klowden has noticed that children usually use the crayons to draw pictures, and adults usually use the crayons to play games.

Klowden says the most interesting drawings he sees usually come on Valentine's Day, a holiday that celebrates romantic love. On that day, the crayons are used for romantic messages and for pictures of hearts and flowers. Klowden says he even saw a crayon message on the tablecloth from one man asking his girlfriend to marry him!

Are you surprised that a restaurant keeps crayons and paper tablecloths on their tables? How do you think you would use the crayons? Why do you think the owner keeps the crayons for his customers?

Personal Creations: Using the Creative Process

This class activity invites you to choose a partner and to create a game together.

Pretend that you and your partner work for a company that designs children's games. Your supervisor gives you a gameboard (the square with different shapes below) and asks both of you to work together and to make a game that the company can sell to children.

With your partner, look over the following gameboard* and begin thinking about ways you can develop a game with the board.

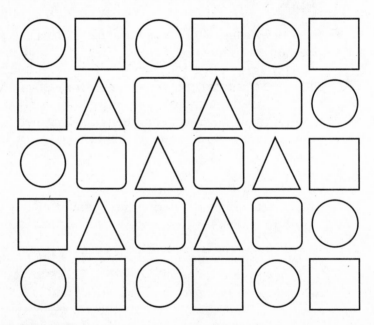

After discussing this gameboard in general, work together to answer the following questions:

* Used with permission of Carole Allen, creativity instructor for Accelerated Learning Forum.

1. What is the name of your game?

2. How many players can play the game at one time?

3. Is there a time limit for each player?

4. How many chances does each player have to try to win?

5. How does a player win points or win the game?

6. Is more equipment needed to play the game? What else do you need?

7. What colors do you want the shapes on the board to be?

8. What language is used in the game?

You will have 25 minutes to design the game. After that, your teacher will ask you or your partner to describe to the class how to play your game. Have fun!

Reflections: About Color

One wonderful thing about crayons is that there are so many different colors to choose between. And the way we use color in pictures, clothes, and decorations is a very important part of any creation.

Colors are also used for different things in different cultures. For example, in both the Chinese and the American cultures, the color black is used during sad times—such as when someone dies. In the United States, the color blue is used as a symbol for both happy and unhappy occasions. When the "bluebird of happiness" comes to your house, it means that your life will be filled with happy things. On the other hand, there is a type of American jazz music called "the blues," and this music is played and sung by people who are feeling sad, lonely, or upset about something. In the Chinese culture blue also has more than one meaning. It is often used as a symbol of death, and it is also used as a symbol for the sky.

In your culture, are the colors black and blue used for different celebrations or ceremonies? What other colors have special meanings in your culture? Describe these colors and their meanings to your partner.

Dictation

Listen to the tape and fill in the missing words.

Good _____ finally put their resources together and made
themselves a _____ . Me, I'm the _____ in the deal.
And I take my job _____ . I introduced him to _____ .
I bought the _____ beginner set—the short, fat, thick ones
with _____ _____ . Every few weeks I would put one in
his _____ and show him how to make a _____ with it. Mostly he
just held it and _____ at me. He had a cigar in his other _____
and couldn't tell the difference between _____ and the Crayola.

Speaking of Culture

Developing a creative imagination for oneself and one's children is very
important to Americans. It is so important that many American parents
expect teachers in preschools (schools for children younger than 4-1/2 or
5 years old) to help develop creativity in their children. At home, many
parents try to do the same thing by using special educational toys,
music, and art. They want their children to feel confident in their own
abilities and to use all their special creative talents.

The following conversation is between Mr. Cooper, a preschool teacher,
and Michio, a college English student who will be working as a teacher's
aide in Mr. Cooper's classroom for the semester. It is Michio's first day at
the preschool.

Mr. Cooper: Michio, since this is your first day here, why don't you
                just see how we do things today and meet the children
                in the class.

Michio: That sounds like a good idea.

It's 8:00 A.M. and time for the class to begin. The children all start
running into the room in different directions, saying hello to the teacher
and other classmates. They hang up their coats and put their lunches on
a table in the back of the room. Mr. Cooper asks all the children to sit
down at the tables.

Michio and the children say hello to each other.

Mr. Cooper	(*to the children*): Since this is Michio's first day here, I'd like you all to draw a picture for him about some of the activities we do here—like drawing, painting, singing, and reading. Get your crayons from the boxes and some drawing paper, and start your pictures.

The children run to their supply boxes to get crayons and drawing paper. Some students return to the tables, and some students sit on the floor to begin drawing the pictures. While they work, they often get up and visit other children and then go back to working on their pictures. Mr. Cooper walks around the room, talks to the children, and looks at their pictures. Michio follows Mr. Cooper. Mr. Cooper says something nice about each picture he sees.

Mr. Cooper	(*talking to individual students*): Nathan, that's a nice color you used for the dog. Rose, that's a wonderful way to draw a flower. Jo Anne, your faces are so interesting.
Michio:	Mr. Cooper, can I ask something?
Mr. Cooper:	Sure.
Michio:	Why did you tell Jo Anne the faces were "interesting"? She made all the faces green.
Mr. Cooper:	In Jo Anne's imagination, the faces are green.
Michio:	And it's so noisy in here. Why don't you tell the students to sit quietly in their seats?
Mr. Cooper:	Children naturally like to move around and talk and draw. It helps feed their imagination and interest. They get a lot of ideas from sharing with other students.
Michio:	In Japan, when students come into a classroom, they walk quietly in one straight line and go directly to their seats. All this noise does not show respect for the teacher.
Mr. Cooper:	One of the most important things we teach here is for the students to have respect for themselves. If they have respect for themselves, they naturally will respect other people.
Michio:	Well, why didn't you draw a picture on the blackboard so the children can copy it? All their drawings are very different and not so good.

Mr. Cooper:	What do you mean, "not so good"?
Michio:	They don't look like anything real. Green faces and purple dogs.
Mr. Cooper:	First, Americans let the children explore their abilities. If they all draw the same picture, they will not have a chance to explore their own mind. After they get used to exploring, they can begin to trust their own thinking. As there is more than one way to draw a picture, there is also more than one way to look at problems and how to solve them. Creative children become creative adults who can see one thing in many ways.
Michio:	I can see that there are a lot of new things here for me to learn and understand. Thanks for the opportunity to work with you.
Mr. Cooper:	I appreciate your help. Now let's go look at some more pictures.

Now answer these questions.

1. Why do you think Michio was surprised at the way the children did things in Mr. Cooper's class?

2. When you went to school, did your teacher follow the ideas of Michio or of Mr. Cooper?

3. If you were going to teach preschool, do you think you would try to follow the idea of Michio or of Mr. Cooper? Describe how you would plan a drawing lesson.

Chapter 10

SUNRISE, SUNSET

Sunrise, sunset
Swiftly go the years.
One season following another -
Bringing its happiness and tears.

> *Adapted from Jerry Bock and Sheldon*
> *Harnick's Fiddler on the Roof*

*L*ook at the chapter title, the picture, and the quotation above the picture. What do you think this chapter is about? What does the picture tell you about the subject?

*C*hapter Preview

About Life's Seasons

Throughout this book, we have looked at many ways various cultures around the world are different from one another. This chapter looks at a unique way in which all humans are the same. No matter where we are born, who are parents are, or what the color of our skin is, each of us follows the same life cycle that consists of birth, development, aging, and death.

Often people speak of these life cycles as "seasons." Just like nature's changing seasons, each human life touches the experiences of spring, summer, fall, and winter. We are continually reminded of these passing life seasons when a child is born or when someone we love dies. These common human experiences and the knowledge that each of us must die someday unite all people around the world.

Interviewing Your Partner

Sit in groups of four students. Name each member of the group in the following way: Student A, Student B, Student C, and Student D. Students A and B should interview each other. Students C and D should interview each other.

Ask your partner the following interview questions and take notes on the answers.

1. Think about your cultural traditions and celebrations. Are any of them related to the seasons, spring to summer, summer to fall, etc.? Which ones are they? Which ones do you enjoy the most? Why?

   _____

   _____

2. Every society has ways to mark the beginnings and the ends of life. In your tradition, how do people celebrate the birth of a new baby? What customs mark the end of someone's life?

_____

_____

3. Many traditions teach that there is a form of life after death. Some people believe that after you die, there is a place you go (like heaven or hell). Other people believe that the soul never dies and moves from body to body. What beliefs about this subject are common in your tradition? What are your personal beliefs about this?

_____

_____

4. It has been said that because no one lives forever, our life has meaning. People who believe this say that if we lived forever, it would take meaning out of our life. Do you think knowing that our life is temporary helps us appreciate life more and adds meaning also?

_____

_____

5. Some very popular international symbols—such as the oriental yin and yang symbols—are frequently used to show life's cycles. What other symbols that show life's cycles have you seen or heard about? Draw them for your partner to see.

_____

_____

Reporting Your Information to the Group

Read over the notes you took about your partner. Then tell the group all about your partner's answers.

Telling or Writing the Group Report

(Optional)

Follow the instructions for this exercise in Chapter 1 (pages 5–6).

$\mathcal{V}$ocabulary Preview (Part I)

Words and Phrases

Before listening to the essay, let's preview some specific vocabulary words you will hear. In this section, each new vocabulary word is listed with its definition beside it, followed by a sample sentence containing the new word or words. If a sample sentence is taken directly from the essay you will hear, the sentence is marked with quotation marks.

Because this chapter's essay has many new vocabulary words and is longer than the others in the book, the activities are divided into two parts.

WORDS or PHRASES	MEANING
1. slabs	large pieces of something (Example: "Its structure is simple—three **slabs** of smooth gray granite, each six inches thick.")
2. granite	a type of stone (Example: Many stone buildings are made of **granite**.)
3. compass	an instrument that tells what direction you are facing—north, south, east, or west (Example: The sailor checked his **compass** to be sure he was going toward the south.)
4. to be aligned	to be set up in a particular direction (Example: "Having checked with a compass to be certain, I can tell that the bench has been carefully **aligned**, so its long sides face east and west and its two end points face north and south.")

WORDS or PHRASES	MEANING
5. sturdy	very strong
	(Example: He bought a **sturdy** chair that would last a long time.)
6. purpose	a reason
	(Example: "This sturdy seat was placed with **purpose** on the highest ground on the highest hill in my city.")
7. tombstone	a stone marker above a grave
	(Example: We saw a very old **tombstone** in the cemetery.)
8. epitaph	words cut into the tombstone
	(Example: His one-sentence **epitaph** described his life.)
9. burial grounds	places where people are buried
	(Example: He directed us to the tombstone in the **burial grounds**.)
10. a paved lane	a short street covered with material to make driving smoother
	(Example: "It's right on the edge of **a paved lane** that curves through the burial grounds.")
11. a worthy companion	a good friend
	(Example: "The closest living thing is a dawn redwood tree—a stout and **worthy companion**.")
12. consciousness	being aware of or knowing something
	(Example: The bench was put there with great **consciousness**.)

13. generosity   sharing with or giving readily to
                                    other people

                                    (Example: He was a person of great
                                    generosity.)

14. a parting gesture   the last action a person makes before
                                    leaving

                                    (Example: "**A parting gesture** of quiet
                                    generosity has been made.")

Vocabulary Quick-Check Review (Part I)

Check your understanding of the new words and phrases introduced
in this chapter by matching the words in column A with their closest
definition in Column B.

Column A	Column B
1. ____ tombstone	a. very strong
2. ____ epitaph	b. an instrument that tells whether you are facing north, south, east, or west
3. ____ slabs	c. short street
4. ____ generosity	d. the last action a person makes before leaving
5. ____ compass	e. large pieces of something
6. ____ purpose	f. stone
7. ____ a parting gesture	g. place where people are buried
8. ____ consciousness	h. a good friend
9. ____ sturdy	i. go in a particular direction
10. ____ a worthy companion	j. a stone marker above a grave
11. ____ granite	k. a reason
12. ____ to be aligned	l. sharing or giving easily to others
13. ____ burial grounds	m. being aware of or knowing something
14. ____ paved lane	n. words that are cut into a tombstone

$\mathcal{E}$ssay Preview (Part I)

This chapter's essay focuses on an unusual bench in a very unusual place. Fulghum goes to this location often to sit on the bench because it is very peaceful there. The bench is located on the highest hill in the city, and on a clear day, he can see 60 miles in three directions. The bench is made of stone, and someone has chiseled (cut into the stone) the following short poem.

> West lies Puget Sound*—
>> East the mighty Cascades** run free—
> North is the University,—
>> South, a great tree.
> All these things were loved by me.

Where do you think this bench is located?

$\mathcal{F}$ocused Listening (Part I)

Look over the following questions before you listen to the tape. This will give you an idea of what information to focus on while listening to the essay the first time. The title and the section of each part you will listen to will be announced on the tape. Listen carefully to each listening section, and then circle the correct answer for each question in that section.

What's This Story About?

SECTION A

1. The bench in the city where he lives contains
   a. three pieces of wood.
   b. three slabs of smooth gray granite.

2. The two supporting legs are
   a. 16 feet high.
   b. 16 inches high.

---

* Puget Sound—a body of water 100 miles long that flows south from the Pacific Ocean past Seattle and Tacoma, Washington, and ends at Olympia, Washington.

** The Cascades—a chain of large mountains that run through the western states of California, Oregon, and Washington.

3. He knows the bench has been perfectly aligned because he
   a. used a compass to check it.
   b. measured it with a ruler.

SECTION B

4. The bench is placed
   a. near the water.
   b. on the highest ground in the city.

5. On a clear day, you can see
   a. almost 60 miles in three directions.
   b. almost 100 miles in three directions.

6. The short poem on the bench talks about
   a. the city and all the things one person loves.
   b. being a student.

SECTION C

7. The words on the bench are
   a. an epitaph.
   b. somebody's name.

8. The bench is really a
   a. tombstone.
   b. picnic bench.

9. The bench is on the edge
   a. of a mountain.
   b. of a paved lane

10. The bench is also located close to a
    a. pine tree.
    b. big redwood tree.

11. Fulghum says this tree is
    a. in the wrong place.
    b. a worthy companion.

12. The person who had the bench built after he or she died did it to be
    a. useful to other people.
    b. famous.

Listen again and check your answers. Share your answers with your partner. Then check your answers with the whole class and discuss any differences of opinion.

Listen Again

In this listening section, you will listen to the complete essay again, but this time there will be no pauses or narration between each section.

The sentences below contain information about the essay you just heard. In every sentence, there is some information that is not true about the essay. The incorrect information is underlined. The sentences are listed in the order that the information is heard on the tape. As you listen to the essay again, cross out the incorrect information and write the correct information above it.

Here are the sentences for you to change. Get ready to focus on the correct answer as you listen to the tape again.

1. Fulghum says there is a bench in the city where he visits.

2. This bench is made of smooth wood.

3. The long sides of the bench face north and south.

4. The seat was placed on the lowest hill in the city.

5. If the sky is clear, you can see in six directions.

6. The words on the edge of the bench are an idiom.

7. Fulghum says that you wouldn't feel comfortable sitting on the bench.

8. Fulghum thinks that the bench shows someone wanted to be useless in death.

Listen to the tape again and check your answers with the rest of the class.

Class Activities

What Do You Think?

Discuss with your class the answers to the following questions.

1. What does the bench look like?
2. Where is it located?
3. Why does Fulghum think that everyone would feel comfortable sitting on the bench? Do you agree or disagree? Why or why not?
4. What is the closest living thing near the bench?
5. Why does Fulghum say that the person who had the bench made and put in that location did it because he or she wanted to leave something useful for other people after he or she died?

Vocabulary Preview (Part II)

Words and Phrases

Before listening to the rest of the essay, let's preview some specific vocabulary words you will hear.

WORDS or PHRASES	MEANING
1. clergyman/woman	a person who is the leader of a religious group—such as a priest, minister, rabbi, or mullah (Example: I have been a **clergyman** for over 25 years.)
2. an identity	who you are (Example: Do you know that woman's **identity**?)
3. narcissism	focusing only on yourself (Example: He never got married because his narcissism was too great.)

WORDS or PHRASES	MEANING
4. a monument	a statue or building built to honor someone who has died
	(Example: They built a **monument** for Abraham Lincoln in Washington, D.C.)
5. conventional	describing something that is usual
	(Example: Her life was very **conventional**.)
6. a spiritual retreat	a quiet place to go for thinking or meditation
	(Example: "That bench has become **a spiritual retreat** for me over the years.")
7. abstract intellectual knowledge	knowing about something as an idea but not as an experience
	(Example: "And it was on that bench, the summer morning after my fiftieth birthday, that I came to that moment in life when one crosses over from the **abstract intellectual knowledge** that all human beings die to the active realization that I will die.")
8. moment of enlightenment	a moment when you suddenly understand something that you didn't understand before
	(Example: "I connect that **moment of enlightenment** with the peculiar sanctuary of the bench and whoever provided it.")
9. sanctuary	a safe place
	(Example: The church was a **sanctuary** during the war.

10. benefactor   a person who gains something from another person's generosity

(Example: When my brother donated money to help me go to college, he became my **benefactor**.)

11. real estate   a house or building on a piece of land or a piece of land

(Example: "I accept the challenge of my unknown benefactor to also leave behind some gift for the living instead of a useless stone marking personal **real estate**.")

Vocabulary Quick-Check Review (Part II)

Check your understanding of the new words and phrases introduced in this chapter by matching the words in column A with their closest definition in Column B.

Column A	Column B
1. ____ a monument	a. usual
2. ____ clergyman or clergywoman	b. a person who gains from someone's generosity
3. ____ moment of enlightenment	c. knowing about an idea but never experiencing it
4. ____ conventional	d. focus on self
5. ____ an identity	e. a building, house, or piece of land
6. ____ sanctuary	f. who you are
7. ____ abstract intellectual knowledge	g. a moment when you suddenly understand something for the first time
8. ____ benefactor	h. a person who donates money for a good purpose
9. ____ a spritual retreat	i. a safe place
10. ____ real estate	j. a statue or building for honoring someone who has died
11. ____ narcisssism	k. a quiet place where you can think

$\mathcal{E}$ssay Preview (Part II)

In this section of the essay, Fulghum tells us about his personal relationship with this bench and the inspiration, pleasure, and lessons he has received while sitting on it.

$\mathcal{F}$ocused Listening (Part II)

Look over the following questions before you listen to the tape. This will give you an idea of what information to focus on while listening to the essay the first time. The title and the section of each part you will listen to will be announced on the tape. Listen carefully to each listening section, and then circle the correct answer for each question in that section.

What's This Story About?

SECTION A

1. Fulghum has been a clergyman for
   a. 25 years.
   b. 45 years.

2. Fulghum says that when people talk about the way they want things after they die, he notices that they often
   a. think only of other family members.
   b. focus a lot only on themselves.

3. Fulghum thinks this narcisssism is a very human
   a. angry feeling.
   b. holding on.

4. To Fulghum, tombstones are markers
   a. of loneliness.
   b. of happiness.

SECTION B

5. Fulghum says that this bench is different from other tombstones because it doesn't have
   a. a name on it.
   b. any place to sit.

6. Fulghum says that in all the cemeteries he has visited around the world, he has seen
   a. many benches like it.
   b. nothing like it.

7. Fulghum says the bench has become
   a. a spiritual retreat for him.
   b. a good place to have conversations with friends.

8. Fulghum says that a young man and a young woman meet at the bench sometimes because
   a. he saw them.
   b. he found a written note taped under the bench.

9. When Fulghum shared the bench with strangers, they
   a. had a long conversation.
   b. didn't speak.

SECTION C

10. On his fiftieth birthday, while sitting on this bench, Fulghum realized that
    a. he was sitting there too long.
    b. he, too, would die some day.

11. Even though it was a moment of awakening, he walked away feeling
    a. OK.
    b. upset.

SECTION D

12. Fulghum connects the moment of enlightenment—when he realized he would die someday—with
    a. the love letter under the bench.
    b. the bench and its benefactor.

13. Fulghum decided that when he dies, he wants
    a. to have a big tombstone built for him.
    b. to leave something useful for other people.

14. Fulghum thinks this bench
    a. will last only a short time.
    b. will last hundreds of years.

15. Fulghum says that for many years in the future, people will sit on that bench and think about
    a. the mysteries of life and death.
    b. how to make more money.

Listen again and check your answers. Share your answers with your partner. Then check your answers with the whole class and discuss any differences of opinion.

Listen Again

In this listening section, you will listen to the complete essay again, but this time there will be no pauses or narration between each section.

The sentences below contain information about the essay you just heard. In every sentence, there is some information that is not true about the essay. The incorrect information is <u>underlined</u>. The sentences are listed in the order that the information is heard on the tape. As you listen to the essay again, cross out the incorrect information and write the correct information above it.

Here are the sentences for you to change. Get ready to focus on the correct answer as you listen to the tape again.

1. Fulghum has been a <u>librarian</u> for twenty-five years.

2. Fulghum says he has been involved in many <u>weddings</u>.

3. Fulghum says that many people focus on <u>others</u> when they think about their own death.

4. Fulghum thinks that tombstones are markers of <u>happiness</u>.

5. Fulghum says that of all the cemetery benches he has seen, he's seen nothing so <u>terrible</u>.

6. For Fulghum, the bench has become a <u>depressing</u> retreat.

7. When Fulghum twice shared the bench with strangers, they all were <u>talking</u>.

8. When Fulghum realized that he, too, would die, he felt <u>terrible</u>.

Listen to the tape again and check your answers with the rest of the class.

Class Activities (Part II)

What Do You Think?

Discuss with your class the answers to the following questions.

1. Why do you think Fulghum says that when people prepare for their death, they focus a lot on themselves? Do you agree or disagree with this idea? Why ?

2. Why do you think that Fulghum calls tombstones "markers of loneliness"? What do you think about this idea?

3. Why does Fulghum think this bench is different than other tombstones?

4. How does Fulghum know that other people also sit on this bench?

5. Do you think that Fulghum admired the person who had the bench built? Why?

Personal Creations: Recipe for a Long Life

Scientists have studied the food and lifestyle habits of people who live very long lives. They have many ideas about what the healthiest lifestyle is, but they still disagree about which one is the best.

Think about your own ideas on the best way to have a long and healthy life. Create a "recipe list" containing all the ingredients you think are necessary. Use the following form to insert your ideas. Then, share your "recipe" with your partner.

Example: Recipe for a Long Life

Ingredients

1. Eat one apple every day.

2. Sleep at least eight hours a day.

3. Take a walk every day.

Now it's your turn.

Recipe for a Long Life, by _____
(Write your name here)

Ingredients

1. _____

2. _____

3. _____

4. _____

5. _____

Reflections: Sharing Ideas Across Cultures

The pages of history books are filled with examples of people who explored places all over the world looking for a "fountain of youth"—or a way of staying young forever. Ancient kings and queens paid much money to men interested in the search for an herb, a plant, or some kind of water that would prevent the natural process of aging.

We do not have to look to ancient history for these examples. Right now in the United States, some laboratories freeze people after they die and plan to keep them frozen until a way is found to bring life again to these people. It's an expensive thing to do, but several people are already frozen, and others have requested freezing after they die.

Is it popular in your culture to try to look young at any age? Do you think that laboratories that freeze people and bring them back to life would be popular in your country? Why or why not?

What do you think about this idea? Would you want to be brought back to life in another time after you die? What about the idea of living forever?

Pretend that you had the opportunity to buy an inexpensive product that would add at least another 100 years to your life. Do you think you would buy it? Why or why not?

Dictation

Listen and fill in the missing words.

There is a _____ in the city where I live.

Its _____ is very simple—just three _____

of smooth gray _____ , each six inches

thick. The ____ part is _____ inches wide by

forty-two inches long. The two supporting legs are

sixteen inches high. Having checked with a

_____ to be certain, I can tell you that the

bench has been carefully _____ so that its

long sides face ____ and west and its two ends

point _____ and south.

Speaking of Culture

The U. S. culture puts a lot of emphasis on staying young and being active. Many senior citizens (people over 60 years old) live long, healthy lives and are expected to be active, interested members of society all their lives. This is often surprising to immigrants and visitors who have just arrived here in the United States.

Here's a conversation between Fusako, a Japanese student who is visiting the United States with her husband for a few years, and her American neighbor Lucille.

Fusako:	Hi, Lucille. Have you got any plans for this weekend?
Lucille:	Oh. Hi, Fusako. My husband and I are planning to help my father move tomorrow.
Fusako:	He's coming to live with you?
Lucille:	No. He's moving from his house to an apartment.
Fusako:	He's going to live by himself? (Fusako is surprised by this.)
Lucille:	Sure. Why not?
Fusakao:	How old is he?
Lucille:	He's 73 years old. You see, my mother died a few years ago when she and my father were still living in the big house the whole family grew up in. My father is a pretty active guy, but he just can't take care of the house and garden by himself anymore.
Fusako:	But why isn't he coming to live with you?
Lucille:	We all talked about that, but there was a problem. My father really needs a lot of quiet, and my three kids are pretty noisy. And since my husband and I both work and all the kids go to school, he would be spending a lot of time alone, anyway.
Fusako:	But what will your father do in the apartment by himself?
Lucille:	He's really not home that much, either. He belongs to a Senior Citizen Center nearby, and he goes there every day to meet his friends, play cards, and sometimes have lunch. He's also taking a carpentry class at the Adult School one night a week.
Fusako:	Your father is 73 and he goes to school? I never heard about anything like that.
Lucille:	I guess we have different expectations here for our senior citizens. We believe no matter what your age or ability, you have the right to continue learning.

Fusako:	Life here is so different from what I knew before. It's a little embarassing for me to say, but before I came here, I heard that the children threw their old parents out on the street. I thought the children didn't love their parents because they didn't live together.
Lucille:	Fusako, the way it is in the United States today is really very different from one or two generations ago. In the past, families stayed together and usually lived in the same town all their lives. At that time, the United States was mostly a country of farms. After railroads and factories were built, people had to leave town to get jobs in other places because many of the farms couldn't make enough money. Also, many young people had to leave their small towns to get an education because most of the colleges were in the cities. After college, some of the students got jobs in that same city, and they stayed there for the better opportunities. The American lifestyle changed at that time to fit the country's changing economy and expectations.
Fusako:	Lucille, you really helped me understand a lot. Thanks.
Lucille:	It was my pleasure. Why don't you and your husband come over to our house on Sunday afternoon. My father will be visiting us then.
Fusako:	That's very nice of you to ask. We'd love to come!

Now answer these questions.

1. How are senior citizens treated in your culture? Do they usually live with their families or by themselves?

2. Are senior citizens in your culture expected to stay active all their life, or is there a different expectation?

3. In your country, is there a retirement program provided by the government or a person's employer? Explain what it is.

4. In your own life, did elderly relatives live with you? What are the good things about the elderly living with their families? Can you think of any bad things about them living with their families?

5. In your mind, what's the best lifestyle for senior citizens?

Tapescript

Chapter 1

It All Started in Kindergarten

Each spring, for many years, I have set myself the task of considering a personal statement of belief: a Credo. My Credo sounds like this: Most of what I really need to know about how to live and what to do and how to be I learned in kindergarten. Wisdom was not at the top of the graduate-school mountain, but there in the sandpile at Sunday School. And these are the things I learned there:

Share everything.

Play fair.

Don't hit people.

Put things back where you found them.

Clean up your own mess.

Don't take things that aren't yours.

Say you're sorry when you hurt somebody.

Wash your hands before you eat.

Flush the toilet after you use it.

I learned that warm cookies and cold milk are good for you.

I learned to live a balanced life—to learn some and think some and draw some and paint and dance and play and work some every day.

And then to take a nap every afternoon.

When you go out into the world, watch for traffic, hold hands and stick together.

I learned to be aware of wonder. Remember the little seed in the Styrofoam cup: The roots go down, the plant goes up, and nobody really knows how or why, but we are all like that.

Goldfish and hamsters and white mice and even the little seed in the Styrofoam cup—they all die. And so do we.

And then I remember the book *Dick and Jane* and the first word I learned—the biggest word of all—LOOK.

Everything you need to know is in there somewhere. The Golden Rule and love and basic sanitation. Ecology and politics and equality and sane living.

You could take any one of those items and extrapolate into sophisticated adult terms and apply them to your family life or your work or your government or your world and they hold true and clear and firm. For example, think what a better world it would be if we all—the whole world—had cookies and milk about three o'clock every afternoon and then lay down with our blankies for a nap. Or if all governments had as a basic policy to always put things back where they found them and to clean up their own mess.

And it is still true, no matter how old you are—when you go out into the world, it is best to hold hands and stick together.

Chapter 2

All Things Are Connected

In the Solomon Islands in the South Pacific some villagers practice a unique form of logging. If a tree is too large to be felled with an ax, the natives cut it down by yelling at it. (*I can't lay my hands on the article, but I swear I read it in a book somewhere.*) You see, woodsmen with special powers creep up on a tree just at dawn and suddenly scream at it at the top of their lungs. They continue this for thirty days. And the tree dies and falls over. The theory is that the hollering kills the spirit of the tree. According to the villagers, it always works.

Me? Well, I yell at my wife. And yell at the telephone and the lawn mower. And yell at the TV and the newspaper and my children. I've been known to shake my fist and yell at the sky at times.

And the man next door, he yells at his car a lot. This summer I heard him yell at a stepladder for most of an afternoon. Modern, urban, educated folks yell at traffic and umpires and bills and banks and machines—especially machines. Machines and relatives get most of the yelling, I suppose.

I don't know what good it does. The machines and the things they just sit there. Even kicking doesn't always help. As for people, well, the Solomon Islanders may have a point. Yelling at living things does tend to kill the spirit in them. Sticks and stones may break our bones, but words will break our hearts. . . .

Chapter 3

What's So Funny?

A troubled man paid a visit to his rabbi. A wise and good old rabbi, as all rabbis try to be. "Rabbi," said he, wringing his hands, "I am a failure. More than half the time I do not succeed in doing what I must do."

"Oh?" said the rabbi.

"Please say something wise, rabbi," said the man.

After much pondering, the rabbi spoke as follows. "Ah, my son, I give you this wisdom: Go and look on page 930 of *The New York Times Almanac* for the year 1970, and you will find peace of mind maybe."

"Ah," said the man, and he went away and did that thing.

Now this is what he found: The listing of the lifetime batting averages of all the greatest baseball players. Ty Cobb, the greatest slugger of them all, had a lifetime average of only point three six seven. Even Babe Ruth didn't do so good.

So the man went back to the rabbi and said in a questioning tone: "Ty Cobb—.367—that's it?"

"Right," said the rabbi. "Ty Cobb—.367. He got a hit once out of every three times at bat. He didn't even bat .500—so what can *you* expect already?"

"Ah," said the man, who thought he was a wretched failure because only half the time he did not succeed at what he must do.

Theology is amazing, and holy books abound.

Chapter 4

Not Quite Yet

Americans, it is observed, prefer definite answers. Let your yea-yea be your yea-yea, and your nay-nay be your nay-nay. Yes or no. No grays please.

In Indonesia, however, there is a word in common use that nicely wires around the need for blacks and whites. *Belum* is the word and it means "not quite yet." A lovely word implying continuing possibility. "Do you speak English?" "*Belum.*" Not quite yet. "Do you have any children?" "*Belum.*" "Do you know the meaning of life?" "*Belum.*" It is considered both impolite and cynical to say "No" outright to important questions. This leads to some funny moments. "Is the taxi on fire?" "*Belum.*" Not quite yet.

Perhaps. Maybe. Possibly. Not yes or no, but within the realm of what might be. Soft edges are welcome in this great bus ride of human adventure.

Is this the best of all possible worlds? *Belum.* Not quite yet.

Is the world coming to an end? *Belum.*

Will we live happily ever after? *Belum.*

Can we do without the weapons of war?

I don't know, we never tried.

Is it hopeless to think we might?

Belum. Not yet.

Chapter 5

Good News

How about some good news for a change? Something to consider when you are in a people-are-no-damn-good mood?

Here's a phrase we hear a lot: "You can't trust anybody anymore." Doctors and politicians and merchants and salesmen. They're all out to rip you off, right?

Well, it ain't necessarily so.

A man named Steven Brill tested the theory. In New York with taxicab drivers. Brill posed as a well-to-do foreigner with little knowledge of English. And he got into several dozen taxis around New York to see how many drivers would cheat him. His friends predicted in advance that most would take advantage of him in some way.

Well, one driver out of thirty-seven actually cheated him. And the rest took him directly to his destination and charged him correctly. Several refused to take him when his destination was only a block or two away, even getting out of their cabs to show him how close he already was. And the greatest irony of all was that several drivers warned him that New York was full of crooks and to be careful.

You will continue to read stories of crookedness and corruption—of policemen who lie and steal, doctors who reap where they do not sew, and politicians on the take. But don't be misled. They are news because they are the exceptions. The evidence suggests that you can trust a lot more people than you think. And the evidence suggests that a lot of people believe that. A recent survey by Gallup indicates that 70 percent of the people believe that most people can be trusted most of the time.

Who says people are no damn good? What kind of talk is that?

Chapter 6

Advice

What I am about to say fits in someplace between the Ten Commandments and Murphy's Law.

God, you will recall, invited old Moses up on a tall mountain in the desert and handed him a couple of solid-gold memos with some powerful words on them. Commandments. God didn't say, "Hey, here are ten pretty good ideas, see what you think." No. Commandments. Do it or take the consequences.

Murphy, at the other extreme, was the ultimate good-humored human cynic who said that no matter what you do, it's probably not going to work out very well anyhow. And some people think that Murphy was an optimist.

As a middle ground, I offer Fulghum's Recommendations. These are items not touched on by God or Murphy, really. Neither as ironclad as the first Ten or as despairing as the endless variations on Murphy. And note that there are only nine on my list. I'm still working on the tenth. Or the eleventh, for that matter.

1. Buy lemonade from any kid who is selling.
2. Any time you can vote on anything, vote.
3. Attend the twenty-fifth reunion of your high school class.
4. Choose having time over having money.
5. Always take the scenic route.
6. Give at least something to any beggar who asks. And
7. Give money to all street musicians.
8. Always be someone's valentine. And
9. When the circus comes to town, be there.

Fulghum's Recommendations.

Chapter 7

Everyday Miracles

My grandfather Sam called me up last Tuesday to ask me if I'd take him to a football game. Grandfather likes small-town high school football—Grandfather is a fan of amateurs and small scale. Some people are concerned about how it is that good things happen to bad people, and there are those who are concerned about how bad things happen to good people. But my grandfather is interested in those times when *miracles* happen to ordinary people. Here again, he likes small scale.

Murphy's Law does not always hold, says Grandfather Sam. Every once in a while the fundamental laws of the universe seem to be momentarily suspended, and not only does everything go right, nothing seems to be able to keep it from going right.

Ever drop a glass in the sink when you're washing dishes and have it bounce nine times and not even chip? Or the glass of knocked-over milk that waltzes across the table but doesn't spill; or the deposit that beat your rubber check to the bank because there was a holiday you forgot about; or the lump in your breast that turned out to be benign; and on and on and on.

When small miracles occur for ordinary people, day by ordinary day. When not only did the worst not happen, but maybe nothing much happened at all, or some little piece fell neatly into place. Or the bliss of just what-was-for-a-day when nothing special took place—life just worked.

My grandfather says he blesses God each day when he takes himself off to bed having *eaten* and not *been eaten* once again. Or in the words of his prayer, "Now I lay me down to sleep. In the peace of amateurs, for whom so many blessings flow. I thank you, God, for what went right! Amen."

Chapter 8

The Masks People Wear

In the early dry dark of an October's Saturday evening, the neighborhood children are playing hide-and-seek. How long since I played hide-and-seek? Thirty years; maybe more. I remember how. I could become part of the game in a moment, if invited. But adults don't play hide-and seek. At least not for fun, anyway. Too bad.

Did you ever have a kid in your neighborhood who always hid so good, nobody could find him? We did. After a while we would give up on him and go off, leaving him to rot wherever he was. And sooner or later he would show up, all mad because we didn't keep looking for him. And we would get mad back because he wasn't playing the game the way it was supposed to be played. And he'd say it was hide-and-seek, not hide-and-give-UP, and we'd all yell about who made the rules and who cared about who, anyway, and how we wouldn't play with him anymore if he didn't get it straight and who needed him anyhow, and things like that. Hide-and-seek-and-yell. No matter what, though, the next time he would hide too good again. And he's probably still hidden somewhere, for all I know.

A man I know found out last year he had terminal cancer. He was a doctor. And he knew about dying, and he didn't want to make his family and friends suffer through that with him. So he kept his secret. And he died. And everybody said how brave he was to bear his suffering in silence and not tell everybody, and so on and so forth. But privately his family and friends said how angry they were that he didn't need them, he didn't trust their strength. And it hurt that he didn't say good-bye.

He hid too well. Getting found would have kept him in the game. This is hide-and-seek, grown-up style. Wanting to hide. Needing to be sought. Confused about being found. "I don't want anyone to know." "What will people think?" "I don't want to bother anyone."

Better than hide-and-seek, I like the game called Sardines. In Sardines the person who is It goes and hides, and everybody else goes looking for him. And when you find him, you get in and hide there with him. And then pretty soon everybody is hiding together, all stacked in a small space like puppies in a pile. And pretty soon somebody giggles and somebody laughs and everybody gets found.

"Olly-olly-oxen-free." The kids out in the street are hollering the cry that says "Come on in, wherever you are. It's a new game." And so say I. To all those who have hid too well: *Get found, kid!* Olly-olly-oxen-free.

Chapter 9

The Creative Process

Good friends finally put their resources together and made themselves a child. Me, I'm the godfather in the deal. And I take my job seriously.

I introduced him to Crayolas. I bought the beginner set — the short, fat, thick ones with training wheels. Every few weeks I would put one in his hand and show him how to make a mark with it. Mostly he just held it and stared at me. He had a cigar in his other hand and couldn't tell the difference between it and the Crayola. But finally, last week, I held his hand and made a big red mark with the Crayola on a sheet of newsprint. And WHAM! He got the picture. A light bulb went off in a new room in his head. And he did it again on his own. Now, reports his mother, with a mixture of pleasure and pain, there is no stopping him.

Crayolas plus imagination (the ability to create images) — these make for happiness if you are a child. Amazing things, Crayolas. Some petroleum-based wax, some dye, a little binder—not much to them really. Until you add the imagination. The Binney Company in Pennsylvania makes about two billion of these oleaginous sticks of pleasure every year and exports them to every country in the United Nations. Crayolas are one of the few things the human race has in common. And that green-and-yellow box hasn't changed since 1937. In fact, the only change has been to rename the "flesh" color "peach." That's a sign of progress.

The way I know about "flesh" and "peach" is that, when I bought my godson his trainer set, I indulged myself and bought my very own set of sixty-four. In the big four-section box with the sharpener built right in. I never had my own set of sixty-four before. Seemed like I was always too young or too old to have one. And while I was at it, I bought several other sets. I got one for the kid's mother and father and explained it was theirs, not his.

When you think about it, for sheer bulk there's more art done with Crayolas than with anything else. There must be billions of sheets of paper in every country in the world, in billions of boxes and closets and attics and cupboards, covered with billions of pictures in crayon. The imagination of the human race poured out like a river. Ronald Reagan and Mikhail Gorbachev used crayons, I bet. And so did Fidel and the emperor of Japan and Rajiv Gandhi and Mrs. Thatcher and Mr. Mubarak and maybe even the ayatollah. And just about everybody else you would care to name.

Maybe we should develop a Crayola bomb as our next secret weapon. A happiness weapon. A Beauty Bomb. And every time a crisis developed, we would launch one. It would explode high in the air—explode softly—and send thousands, millions, of little parachutes into the air. Floating down to earth—boxes of Crayolas.

I guess that sounds absurd, doesn't it? Crazy, silly, weird. But I was reading in the paper today how much money the Russians and our Congress have just set aside for weapons. And I think about what those weapons will do. And I'm not confused about what's weird and silly and crazy and absurd. Pass the crayons, please.

Chapter 10

Sunrise, Sunset

There is a bench in the city where I live. Its structure is very simple—just three slabs of smooth gray granite, each six inches thick. The seat part is sixteen inches wide by forty-two inches long. And the two supporting legs are sixteen inches high. Having checked with a compass to be certain, I can tell you that the bench has been carefully aligned so that its long sides face east and west and its two ends point north and south.

This sturdy seat was placed with purpose on the highest ground on the highest hill in my city. So that when the sky is clear on a summer's morning, you can see almost sixty miles in three directions while sitting on the bench.

West lies Puget Sound—
East the mighty Cascades run free—
North is the University—
South, a great tree.
All these things were loved by me.

These words are chiseled into the edge of the bench and are an epitaph. For the bench is, in fact, a tombstone in a cemetery. And I would take you there to sit if I only could.

You wouldn't feel uncomfortable sitting on it, I promise. You wouldn't even notice what it was at first. It's right on the edge of a paved lane that curves through the burial grounds, placed so that you are clearly invited to sit on it. The closest living thing is a dawn redwood tree, comforting in its great age and size—a stout, worthy companion.

The placement of this bench, the words on the edge, the consciousness of the view—all say that someone went to a lot of trouble to be useful in death. A parting gesture of quiet generosity has been made.

In over twenty-five years as a clergyman, I have been involved in hundreds of funerals—in the dying that went before, the burial that came after. There is an inevitable narcissism therein—a focus on self: what I want for MY funeral and what I want done with MY body and what I want for MY epitaph—a very human holding-on to identity as long as breath and granite last. The monuments left behind in the hallowed ground serve to separate the dead from the living and oddly enough the dead from one another. For me, tombstones are markers of loneliness.

But this bench I speak of is another story. It's unique. There's no name. No conventional epitaph. And no dates. Just an unspoken open invitation for anyone to sit and think. What marks this grave is the gift of silent companionship that bridges loneliness. In all the cemeteries I have visited around the world, I have seen nothing like it—and nothing so fine.

That bench has become a spiritual retreat for me over the years. And I know that I am not the only one to use it, for once I found a note taped under the bench. Not for me, but for a young woman from a young man who was in love with her and wrote her careless poetry with great passion.

Twice I have shared the bench with strangers. I can't explain how we each knew the bench was important to the other and that company was welcome. We just knew, that's all. We sat in silence and went our ways.

And it was on that bench, the summer morning after my fiftieth birthday, that I came to that moment in life where one crosses over from the abstract intellectual knowledge that all human beings die to the active realization that I will die. Me. Fulghum. Will not be. Sooner or later.

And not only did I realize that I will die, but I walked away thinking, Well, it's okay.

And I connect that moment of enlightenment with the peculiar sanctuary of that bench and whoever provided it. And I accept the challenge of my unknown benefactor to also leave behind some gift for the living instead of a useless stone marking personal real estate.

That bench will last hundreds of years. Many people will sit on it and think not of the name of its owner but of the nameless joys of this sweet life and the mystery of death and how utterly amazing it all is, and that somehow, in the end, things are just as they should be.